DIFFERENT DESIGNS
WHAT I WISH I KNEW 30 YEARS AGO

DAVID BRYANT

Different Designs
What I Wish I Knew 30 Years Ago
© 2024 David Bryant

ISBN 978-1-954617-84-1 paperback
978-1-954617-85-8 eBook

Yawn's Publishing
678-880-1922
www.yawnspublishing.com

www.yawnspublishing.com

678-880-1922
Canton, Georgia

Printed in the United States of America

CONTENTS

Acknowledgements

I worked with very accomplished and ethical professionals that provided me with guidance throughout my career. To name a few here:

Michael Nowicki
Jack Shapiro
Dave Collins
Gary Grover
David Laird
Jim Burns
Richard Wright

Special Thanks to Erin Abbott for Support and Inspiration.
Photography & Editing Taylor Summer and Taylor Bryant

1

Influence

The influence our ancestors, living or not, have on us always amazes me. Alfred, Lord Tennyson might have put it best in his poem "Ulysses" when he said *"I am a part of all that I have met."* My ethics and sense of right and wrong are mostly a result of what my parents, grandparents believed were the "rules." To their dismay, many of those rules no longer apply, but they have an influence, nonetheless.

In many cases, their rules and values were formed by previous generation. For instance, Depression era parents were very concerned with spending and saving, and who could blame them? They feared losing their jobs, all their savings, and not having enough money to pay for their homes, not having enough to eat or being able to provide for their kids. We can imagine that fear.

How bad did Americans have it? By the time Franklin D. Roosevelt was inaugurated as president in 1933, the banking system had collapsed, nearly 25% of the labor force was unemployed, and prices and productivity had plummeted to one-third of their 1929 levels. This resulted in widespread factory shutdowns, farm and home foreclosures, and significant hunger across the nation. The height of the Depression in 1933 saw 24.9% of the nation's total workforce, or 12,830,000 people, unemployed. Wage income for workers who managed to retain their jobs fell by 42.5% between 1929 and 1933. The displacement of the workforce and farming communities led to families splitting up or migrating in search of work, with many heading to California in hopes of finding better opportunities.

Listen, I believe we all have free will, but at the same point, the era is which we grow up on has a significant impact on our attitudes and personas. Philosopher Baruch de Spinoza, when speaking of hard determinism, once said "Men are deceived because they think themselves free…and the sole reason for thinking so is that they are conscious of their own actions, and ignorant of the causes by which those actions are determined." The fact that I was reared by the silent generation and the Greatest generation led me to the work ethic that has propelled me to have the success I am having today. I have always truly lived out the word of an unknown author when he said, "Duty then is the most sublime word in the English language. You should do your duty in all things. You can never do more, you should never wish to do less."

One day, I recall asking my mom for some gum. She would reach in her purse and tear a stick in half and give one to me and one to my sister. As I matured, I began to understand why she was so frugal. I didn't understand it then, but she was trying to have me live out the words of Henry David Thoreau when he said, "We make ourselves rich by making our wants few." I also think she was training me to become the hospital executive I would become years later. More on that in a little bit. As a form of rebellion, I frequently find myself buying a pack of gum and chewing the whole pack.

I admit, chewing a whole pack of gum is not productive, but some things need to be unlearned. I propose that we have been programmed by those that would have given their lives for us, and we need to deprogram ourselves from living by their rules; after all, Frederick Douglass once said, "It is easier to build strong children than to repair broken men." Still, within their programming are brilliant gems of wisdom, but some of their beliefs can hold you back. We all have different temperaments, talents, and convictions, so what may work for one may not work for another. We will work on separating the gems from the limitations your parents unknowingly gave you.

While I had a great family, I have enjoyed dissecting their influences primarily in the areas of my professional life and how I operate my company. I am sure many members of my family have thought or still think I am bizarre, but I prefer the term bold. But being bold in a professional career can lead to success by encouraging risk-taking, which is often necessary for innovation and leadership. Boldness helps in standing out for promotions or opportunities, as it shows confidence and the ability to handle challenges. It also fosters resilience, enabling individuals to bounce back from setbacks and learn from failures, which is crucial for long-term success. Moreover, bold professionals are more likely to advocate for themselves and their ideas, leading to greater visibility and recognition in their fields.

I was not always as bold as I am now. I stumbled out of Alice High School with a mediocre GPA, yet somehow, Abilene Christian accepted me. Four years later, I received a BA in Mass Communications. Although I was grateful for the education, I had a lot of maturing to do. Ralph Waldo Emerson was certainly right when he quipped, "The years teach much which the days never know."

After wandering around Austin, Texas, working sub-par jobs, I decided to go to graduate school at Southwest Texas State University—now Texas State University—to study Healthcare Administration.

It was one of those moments where a choice is made that affects everything in your life. Those moments are so subtle but so important to recognize and appreciate. I decided to take on a graduate school with no money, but a lot of ambition and maybe a dash of ego. I always realized I had to be super passionate about my career. Steve Jobs has said the same thing when encouraging youth when he said, "Your work is going to fill a large part of your life, and the only way to be truly satisfied is to do what you believe is great work. And the only way to do great work is to love what you do." I didn't want to excel in my career just for the money or status, I wanted to the best I could be so I could not reflect in a positive light on generations that came before me but hold that reflection of excellence for generations that would come after me.

After meeting with the dean of the fairly new graduate program, I was confident I could be successful and get my degree in a couple of years. Before I could be accepted to the program, I had to take a couple of undergraduate classes at a community college—statistics and medical terminology I believe.

I have a powerful memory of standing in line to register for those two classes and realizing I was going to be late for work. Doubt crept up. You know that horrible feeling of 'I'll never be able to pull this off?' That fear? Well, I said to myself, "I am going to do this. I don't care if I am late to work, and I will figure out how to pay for this." For challenging moments like these, I suggest memorizing a quote to not only give you comfort, but to give you strength. The quote that has always come to mind for me is quote that is wrongly attributed to Dr. Martin Luther King Jr. said, "Faith is taking the first step even when you don't see the whole staircase." I've found in my life what is unseen shouldn't scare you but excite you because it involves taking a path that very few or bold enough to take.

Had I not done that, my life would be very different, not necessarily bad, but choosing to take control and commit to getting my degree set me on my path to success. Assuming control over our destinies and dedicating ourselves to achieving a specific outcome stands as one of the most empowering decisions we can undertake.

Although it was challenging, working several jobs, and attending grad school, I have so many fond memories of that era of my life.

Believe it or not, stress is actually good to have if that that stress is eustress and not distress.

Eustress is positive stress that motivates and focuses energy, beneficial for productivity and personal growth. Distress is negative stress that can lead to anxiety, decrease in performance, and health problems. Eustress is important because it encourages us to push our boundaries in a healthy way, leading to improved performance, skill development, and satisfaction from overcoming challenges. The best are not afraid of stress and often ask for more, relishing their innate ability to handle it, while the ones who sit on the side-lines will continue to sit there. An apathetic nature guarantees one thing in life for that person: because they strive for nothing, they get nowhere. It was not a glamorous life but one that involved many tv dinners and ramen. But I felt like I was on fire, taking on the world. What I've realized in life is that things add up over time. The most successful of people build off tiny and early successes, thinking of them as stairs. Stairs make you elevate; they make you get off your feet. So, too, do these tiny and early successes.

School was mainly at night, so I had plenty of time to work and make a little change. One of my jobs was at a Tennis Club, assigning courts, handing out towels, mowing the yard. I loved the job and met so many lovely people. While this type of work might not have mattered to your average person, it mattered a great deal because I was taught that if you do your best at whatever task you have set before you, not only will your superiors notice, but it will ingrain good habits that will be needed in future work.

I believe the reason why I have had so much success in my career is because I am very high in the personality trait conscientiousness. People high in conscientiousness tend to be more disciplined, organized, and goal-oriented. These traits contribute to their ability to plan effectively, persist in the face of obstacles, and manage time and resources efficiently. Their attention to detail and ability to follow through with commitments often lead to higher performance in both academic and professional settings, making them more likely to achieve success compared to those with lower levels of conscientiousness.

One of the tennis players owned an apartment complex in Hyde Park. It was a small 28-unit place, and he said that I could live there free of charge if I would collect rent and show potential renters the vacant apartments. I earned 400 sq. ft. of pure gold. I will always be grateful to that gentleman. You need help from time to have success and you certainly need luck as well. Are the most successful born with more innate talent than others? Yes and no. To get in a position of having success, you have to be born with some amount of talent and get lucky to an extent, but the harder you work and smarter and wiser choices you make, the less than luck or being born with talent in the first-place matters. We all run into good luck from time to time in our lives, but the key thing to remember is that if you prepare on the front end, that luck can catapult you forward in ways you would never have dreamed of. People receive good luck all of the time, but for the most part, they aren't prepared to take advantage of it. For me, I've always been ready to take advantage of it.

On the weekends, I got to put on a suit and tie to work at the business office at St. David's Medical Center. That position was especially enjoyable and where I started to learn about the world of healthcare.

I confess, I had a few angels that helped me along the way. One of my professors was a former executive with Humana back when it still operated hospitals. We had a good relationship. We used to play a little tennis and throw back a beer or two after class. What I've learned throughout my life is that to have success in life, that the old saying "it is isn't the grades you make, but the hands you shake" is 100% accurate. Being high in the personality trait agreeableness is associated with a range of behaviours and attitudes that can significantly contribute to success in the workforce, especially in roles that involve extensive networking. Agreeableness, one of the five major dimensions of personality in the Five Factor Model, refers to an individual's propensity to be cooperative, compassionate, and friendly towards others. Here are several reasons why this trait can lead to success in networking-intensive careers:

Enhanced Interpersonal Relationships:

Agreeable individuals are more likely to be well-liked by their colleagues and clients due to their empathetic and cooperative nature.

8

This popularity can facilitate smoother interactions and stronger professional relationships, which are crucial in networking settings where rapport and trust are key.

Effective Communication:

People high in agreeableness tend to be good listeners and communicators, showing genuine interest in the perspectives and needs of others. This quality can make them more effective in negotiations and in building alliances, as they are seen as understanding and supportive partners.

Conflict Resolution:

Agreeable individuals are typically better at resolving conflicts due to their tendency to seek compromise and to prioritize harmony over personal gains. This trait can be invaluable in maintaining stable, long-term professional relationships and in ensuring collaborative environments.

Teamwork and Collaboration:

The cooperative nature of agreeable people makes them excellent team players. They are often willing to assist colleagues and to contribute positively to team dynamics, making them valuable members of any organization. Their ability to work well with others can lead to successful collaborative efforts and networking opportunities.

Adaptability:

High agreeableness may also correlate with a greater willingness to adapt one's own needs and preferences for the sake of the group or project success. This flexibility can be particularly beneficial in dynamic industries where networking and collaboration with a diverse range of stakeholders are essential.

Building a Broad Network:

Agreeable individuals are more likely to engage in networking activities in a way that feels authentic and non-transactional. Their genuine interest in others can lead to the development of a wide network of contacts who are more likely to reciprocate with opportunities, information, and support.

Positive Reputation:

Being agreeable can contribute to a positive personal and professional reputation. People are more likely to recommend and refer individuals whom they find pleasant, reliable, and cooperative, which can open up new opportunities and facilitate career advancement.

Ultimately, to finish my degree, I had one of two options. One was to author a thesis. I thought, "No way. I'm out." The second was do an internship or residency. As it turned out, Humana had an administrative residency program, and my professor had some influence in choosing talent. Residency was my ideal option as it was essentially training to become an administrator or executive within the company. It satisfied my academic requirement and teed me up my first executive position.

I remember Humana flew me to Newport Beach for my residency interview. I felt like I was on top of the world. As I recall, the interview did not go that well, but apparently, I didn't embarrass myself too badly. They hired me at $28K, which would be around $90K a year today adjusted for inflation and moved me to Denver for my 10-month residency. That was an exciting time in my life. Although my main driver in my career has never been money, it felt nice being able to support myself comfortably; it gave me some sense of control in my life I had never had and something that I knew my relatives had always hoped I would possess. I was able to afford a nice apartment and the position was at an investor-owned company. The department head and senior executives were kind but tough, and while patient care and quality came first, we were expected to provide top notch service and large returns for the investors. I learned organization dynamics, like noticing the behaviour of other employees around me, learned how to read body language, and began to understand what the people managers, responsible for overseeing my training, felt were important. Basically, all the stuff you cannot learn in a textbook, and would only realize by working. Robert Sternberg, a psychology professor at Cornell, has written extensively on what type of intelligence is needed for the workforce. It is called the Triarchic Theory of Intelligence:

It is framework that extends beyond the traditional IQ-based views of intelligence, emphasizing the importance of practical and creative abilities alongside analytical skills. This broader perspective on intelligence has significant implications for the workforce, highlighting the need for a diverse set of cognitive abilities to navigate the complex and dynamic challenges of the modern workplace. Here are several reasons why the Triarchic Theory of Intelligence is important for the workforce:

Analytical Intelligence (Componential):

This aspect of intelligence involves the ability to analyse, evaluate, judge, compare, and contrast. In the workplace, analytical intelligence enables employees to solve problems, make decisions, and process information efficiently. It is crucial for roles that require critical thinking, data analysis, and strategic planning.

Creative Intelligence (Experiential):

Creative intelligence is about the ability to use experience in novel ways, to think in new directions, and to apply existing knowledge to solve new and unique problems. In the workforce, creativity fosters innovation, adaptability, and the development of new products, services, or solutions. It is especially important in industries that are rapidly evolving or in roles that demand thinking outside the box to overcome challenges.

Practical Intelligence (Contextual):

Practical intelligence involves the ability to adapt to, shape, and select environments to meet both personal and organizational goals. It encompasses what is often referred to as "street smarts" or "common sense." In the workplace, practical intelligence is key to navigating the social dynamics of the organization, managing resources effectively, and implementing theoretical knowledge in real-world situations. It is crucial for leadership, management, and roles requiring interpersonal skills and situational awareness.

I have noticed that it has five distinct implications for the workforce:

Holistic Talent Development:

The Triarchic Theory underscores the importance of developing a broad range of cognitive abilities within the workforce. Organizations can benefit from training programs that enhance not just analytical skills but also creativity and practical problem-solving abilities.

Diverse Teams:

Understanding that intelligence is multifaceted supports the creation of diverse teams, where individuals with different cognitive strengths can complement each other, leading to more innovative and effective problem-solving.

Adaptability and Innovation:

In a rapidly changing economic environment, employees with a blend of analytical, creative, and practical intelligence are more adaptable and capable of innovation, helping organizations stay competitive.

Recruitment and Selection:

Incorporating the Triarchic Theory into recruitment and selection processes allows employers to identify candidates with a balance of analytical, creative, and practical skills, potentially leading to more effective and versatile teams.

Leadership Development:

Leaders who exhibit strengths in all three areas of intelligence are likely to be more effective, as they can navigate complex problems, inspire innovation, and adapt their strategies to the changing landscape of the business world.

Anyway, when it was time to go to my first gig as Assistant Executive Director I could feel some momentum within the organization, I figured I could collaborate well with these people. So, off I go to Humana Hospital-Abilene. (More angels involved here but that is for another story for another day.) This was my first gig where were people reporting to me. Most of the department heads I managed were closer to my parent's age. I did a better than average job of respecting their tenure and knowledge, and figured they were happy with my performance. Many had a lot to teach me, quite frankly. Many of the tasks were not particularly enjoyable but I had to have them to gear up for what I do today. I've always said, "to get do what you really want to do, you're going to have to do things you don't really want to do."

Hospitals are some of the most complex organizations because of the diversity of skill sets. I briefly mentioned this earlier when discussing Sternberg's ideas. I think that really great CEOs in administration have mastered the skill of bringing people together toward one vision. Howard Schultz, founder and CEO of Starbucks, once said, "The most powerful and enduring brands are built from the heart. They are real and sustainable. Their foundations are stronger because they are built with the strength of the human spirit, not an ad campaign. The companies that are lasting are those that are authentic." I've found that to be true in any successful company. CEOs of any industry should live out this quote, but it especially true of hospitals because the chief responsibility of a hospital is to care for its patients.

After a couple of years there, I was ready to move on up to an exceptional hospital in Phoenix, Paradise Valley Hospital. At 29 years old, I was the new Chief Operating Officer. It was a fantastic facility, but that was where the grind began. I had a lot of responsibility. Whenever I go through challenging times, I think of this below quote by Thomas Paine:

> *The harder the conflict, the more glorious the triumph. What we obtain too cheap, we esteem too lightly; it is dearness only that gives everything its value. I love the man that can smile in trouble, that can gather strength from distress and grow brave by reflection. 'Tis the business of little minds to shrink; but he whose heart is firm, and whose conscience approves his conduct, will pursue his principles unto death.*

My skills were starting to look good on paper, but more than that, I was getting the confidence to take risks and looking at the prospects of leaving a salary, benefits, 401k, etc. Not *quite* ready to jump, though. Having a young family and a mortgage makes you think long and hard about how aggressive you want to go in the entrepreneurial direction. I knew I wanted more autonomy and control over my financial life, and HCA were the owners. Certainly, HCA was a hall-of-fame healthcare company, and I could have stayed on that path. But I wanted to do things a unique way by a different design. I've always thought of myself as a divergent thinker. Convergent thinking is most often tested in school, but I've learned that throughout my life divergent thinkers are the ones who push the needle forward in any organization.

Divergent Thinking

Definition: Divergent thinking is a thought process used to generate creative ideas by exploring many possible solutions. It involves thinking out of the box and generating multiple answers to a problem from a single starting point.

Characteristics:

Creativity: Emphasizes novel or unique solutions rather than conventional ones.

Open-ended: Involves open-ended questions or problems with multiple possible answers.

Quantity: Encourages the generation of a large number of ideas.

Exploration: Focuses on spreading outwards in various directions to explore different aspects of an issue.

Application:

Divergent thinking is often used in creative processes, brainstorming sessions, and in situations where innovative solutions are required. It's crucial in artistic endeavours, research and development, and any field that values innovation.

Convergent Thinking Definition:

Convergent thinking is a thought process that aims to find a single, correct solution to a problem. It involves applying logical steps and narrowing down the options to converge upon the most effective answer.

Characteristics:

Logical: Relies on logic and systematic steps to reach a solution.

Closed-ended: Deals with problems that have a single, correct answer.

Efficiency: Focuses on determining the most effective and efficient answer to a problem.

Analysis: Involves analyzing and evaluating information to make decisions.

Application: Convergent thinking is utilized in standardized testing, mathematical calculations, decision-making processes that require a definitive answer, and situations where the goal is to solve specific problems efficiently.

Key Differences:

Nature of Solutions:

Divergent thinking seeks multiple, varied solutions, while convergent thinking aims for a single, correct solution.

Process: Divergent thinking involves creative exploration of possibilities, whereas convergent thinking involves logical analysis to narrow down options.

Usage Context:

Divergent thinking is used in creative and open-ended contexts requiring novelty, whereas convergent thinking is applied in contexts needing definitive answers and efficiency.

Problem Type:

Divergent thinking is best for problems that are open and allow for creativity, while convergent thinking is suited for problems that are well-defined and require specific solutions.

But, when we get back to it, I got a position with Universal Health Services, another hall-of-fame healthcare company working in mergers and acquisitions. UHS is where I really got my skills and confidence to leave the W2 safety net. They had top-notch executives and a good corporate team. I was getting firsthand experience in how valuations were assembled and monetized. I got to play with the big boys and learned how they positioned acquisitions and blended them with their existing family of facilities. There were lots of air miles, presentations, and late dinners, but I was beginning to visualize creating my own company and becoming the President and CEO as my last job. Ted Turner once famously said, "confronted with a problem I've always looked for an unconventional angle and approach. Nothing sneaky, nothing illegal or unethical, just turning the issue on its head and shifting the advantage to our side." That's the type of the mentality I knew I had to take, and in the coming chapters, I will tell you just how exactly I did it in hopes that you can follow in my footsteps in whatever endeavour you are trying to undertake.

2

The Balance

Life's greatest challenge faced by any executive or entrepreneur is to maintain a balance as they juggle between having a successful career path, a successful company, and at the same time, the responsibility of raising good children, working, and having a good marriage.

So, a lot of successful people struggle to strike a balance between their personal and professional lives, and I wanted to bring this to people's attention because I did not do very well at this. I remember being selfish, career-oriented, focused on my goal, and only wanting to make money and look good in front of my peers. In terms of work life balance, the best opinion I have ever heard on the subject came from Sheryl Sandberg, the former COO of Facebook: "There's no such thing as work-life balance. There's work, and there's life, and there's no balance."

Unfortunately, I made some work-life choices that were not so good. Being highly focused often benefits one's career, yet it takes a wise individual to ensure that their family does not become neglected in the process. After all, we brought them into this world, and they deserve our undivided love and attention often. In my case, I was not even interested in going to a dance competition with my girls. I would miss family events and prioritize my work over anything, not realizing how huge the opportunity cost of it was to me.

Spending an excessive amount of time at work at the expense of family time can have several psychological repercussions. Here are four to five reasons, from a psychological perspective, why this imbalance can be harmful:

Emotional Disconnect:

Consistently prioritizing work over family can lead to emotional detachment within family relationships. This detachment can manifest as feelings of isolation, misunderstanding, or neglect among family members. The absence of quality time spent together weakens emotional bonds, making it more challenging to maintain close, supportive relationships.

Increased Stress and Anxiety:

The pressure and stress from work can spill over into family life, exacerbating stress levels not just for the individual but also for family members. The individual may experience heightened anxiety about meeting work demands, which can limit their ability to relax and be present during family interactions, leading to a stressed household environment.

Impaired Child Development: Parents who spend excessive time at work may miss out on critical aspects of their children's emotional and psychological development. A lack of parental involvement and support can affect children's self-esteem, academic performance, and can contribute to behavioral problems. Children require consistent engagement from parents for healthy emotional and social development.

Decreased Personal Well-Being:

Neglecting time for family and personal activities can lead to burnout, a state of emotional, physical, and mental exhaustion caused by prolonged stress. When work consumes the majority of an individual's time and energy, it can diminish their sense of personal well-being and satisfaction, potentially leading to depression and a feeling of disconnection from one's personal life.

Relationship Strain:

Excessive work hours can strain intimate relationships and marriages, leading to conflicts, dissatisfaction, and in some cases, separation or divorce. The partner may feel neglected or bear a disproportionate share of household responsibilities, which can erode the foundation of the relationship. Effective communication and shared experiences, critical components of a healthy relationship, are compromised when work takes precedence over family time.

Moreover, there's a critical aspect of balance that leaders must grasp: the importance of stepping away from work, even if it means just playing a round of golf with friends a few times a month. This harmonious integration of professional and personal spheres not only enriches one's life but also opens doors to networking opportunities. By moving away from your desk and venturing into the world, you make yourself available to new connections. No longer are you confined to sitting silently behind your desk all day, isolated from your colleagues—or in my situation, from the hospital doctors.

When you are not taking time out to go watch a play or to treat yourself to a nice dinner with your peers or your family, it really limits you and tightens up your scope. And soon, you will find yourself stuck in monotony. So, while waking up early, working hard in the office, and jamming in and doing the best you can reflect well on your career and work ethic, in the long run, it isn't a sustainable way of living.

Overworking can have detrimental effects on both physical and mental health over time. Here are three to four examples illustrating why excessive work can lead to harm:

Physical Health Decline:

Extended periods of overworking can lead to chronic stress, which is associated with a host of physical health issues including heart disease, hypertension, weakened immune function, and increased risk of stroke. The constant pressure and long hours can also exacerbate lifestyle-related problems such as poor diet and lack of physical activity, further compromising health.

Mental Health Issues:

The psychological toll of overworking is significant. It can lead to increased risks of anxiety, depression, and burnout—a state of emotional, physical, and mental exhaustion. The stress of trying to meet high demands with inadequate recovery time can impair cognitive functions like concentration, memory, and decision-making.

Relationship Strain:

Overworking often means spending less time with family and friends, leading to strained relationships. The absence and emotional unavailability of an overworked individual can erode the foundation of personal relationships, leading to feelings of neglect, resentment, and isolation among loved ones.

Decreased Productivity and Job Satisfaction:

Ironically, while overworking is often driven by a desire to increase productivity and success, it can have the opposite effect over time. Fatigue, stress, and burnout can decrease efficiency, creativity, and overall job performance. Furthermore, the lack of balance can diminish job satisfaction and lead to disengagement from work.

You have also got to blend that piece that is about making yourself physically healthy, eating well, taking care of yourself, paying attention to your loved ones, and looking after your mental health. It is completely all right to work hard in the early days of your career, but someday, you'll realize what's important.

The payoff of maintaining a social life is also having a very vast network of people across all industries. Even though that I was in healthcare, I was still really interested in interacting people that worked in technology. Venturing out and engaging with others offers a fresh, unique perspective, as opposed to remaining in a narrow, insular state, confined to the echo chamber of your own industry.

I think limiting yourself at any stage of your life is the worst mistake you can make. Even Michael Jordan once said, "Limits, like fears, are often just an illusion." I think that when you have a bigger perspective of the world from so many different people, it gives you more clarity and helps you see your own goals clearly. It helps you see things beyond just sitting behind your desk all day and making people think that you are this great, hard-working executive.

Diversity of thought, also known as cognitive diversity, is beneficial for several key reasons, particularly in collaborative environments like workplaces, educational settings, and within communities. Here are some of the main advantages:

Enhanced Creativity and Innovation:

Diverse perspectives encourage the generation of a broader range of ideas and solutions. When individuals with different backgrounds, experiences, and ways of thinking come together, it fosters creativity and can lead to innovative solutions that might not arise in a more homogenous group.

Improved Problem Solving:

Research has shown that diverse groups often outperform more homogenous ones in problem-solving tasks. This is because diverse groups can draw upon a wider variety of viewpoints and approaches, leading to more thorough analysis and better outcomes.

Greater Resilience:

Diversity of thought can contribute to the resilience of teams and organizations. A mix of perspectives can help groups to adapt more readily to change and to navigate challenges more effectively, as they are less likely to be trapped in groupthink or overly reliant on a single approach.

Enhanced Decision Making:

Cognitive diversity can lead to more robust decision-making processes. When different viewpoints are considered, decisions are more likely to take into account a wider range of factors and potential impacts, leading to more balanced and effective outcomes.

Increased Engagement and Inclusion:

Environments that value diversity of thought tend to be more inclusive, making individuals feel valued and respected for their unique contributions. This can lead to higher levels of engagement, satisfaction, and morale among team members or within communities.

Better Reflection of Society: In a globalized world, organizations and communities are more likely to thrive if they reflect the diversity of the society around them. Diversity of thought ensures that a variety of cultural, social, and economic perspectives are represented, which can enhance the relevance and impact of their work.

I think that much of my generation kind of grew up under the hardcore concept of getting to the office as early and leaving as late as you can. But it does not really play out that well. I mean, you must do it to keep your jobs and to gain respect in the industry, but it isn't really in your favor to do it by your heart, forgetting leisure.

Once I got out of Corporate America and started to work on things that were actually productive as opposed to things that were just for optics or for show, is when I felt the most alive. I felt like I was finally doing something for myself and not just slaving away for someone else's organization while ignoring my personal needs. I definitely agree with Jeff Bezos when he said: "One of the only ways to get out of a tight box is to invent your way out." In essence, do not think that you have to stay on this regimented course. In fact, you should expand yourself and write to your friends and colleagues who are from different industries, diverse cultures, and opinions. This is what will truly broaden your horizons as I mentioned earlier.

3

Different Designs

The phrase "different designs" actually comes from an old rock song which was called Grand Designs, but the essence of the song is still relevant. It's not one my favorite tunes, but I still remember this song clearly to this day.

As human beings, we can have a herd mentality. We can exhibit a herd mentality due to a complex interplay of psychological, social, and evolutionary factors. Herd mentality, also known as herd behavior or mob mentality, describes how individuals in a group can be influenced by their peers to adopt certain behaviors follow trends, or make decisions that they might not necessarily make independently. Several key reasons underpin this phenomenon:

Social Conformity:

One of the primary drivers of herd mentality is the deep-rooted human desire to conform to group norms and expectations. Social conformity ensures social cohesion and acceptance within the group, which are crucial for an individual's psychological well-being and social survival. People often conform to avoid standing out, to be liked, or to avoid conflict, leading to a tendency to go along with the group even if it contradicts their personal beliefs or preferences.

Social Learning:

Humans learn behaviors and norms through observation and imitation of others, a process known as social learning. This mechanism allows individuals to rapidly acquire new skills and adapt to their environment by emulating the actions of the majority. In situations where the appropriate behavior is unclear, individuals are more likely to follow the lead of others, assuming that the group's collective behavior is the correct response.

Informational Influence:

In many cases, individuals assume that the group has more information than they do individually, leading them to conform to the group's decisions as a way of making informed choices. This is particularly true in uncertain or ambiguous situations where the correct course of action is not obvious, and people rely on the wisdom of the crowd to guide their decisions.

Fear of Isolation:

Humans are inherently social creatures with a fear of isolation and rejection. The prospect of being socially ostracized or alienated for deviating from the group can be a powerful motivator for individuals to adopt herd behavior, even when it goes against their personal judgments or moral principles.

Evolutionary Perspective:

From an evolutionary standpoint, there is a survival advantage in sticking with the group. Our ancestors who lived in tribes and communities were more likely to survive and reproduce than those who were isolated. Being part of a group provided protection from predators, increased success in hunting and gathering, and enhanced reproductive opportunities. Thus, herd behavior may be hardwired into our psychology as a survival mechanism.

Emotional Contagion:

Emotions can spread rapidly through a group, influencing others to feel and act in similar ways. This emotional contagion can lead to herd behavior, especially in situations charged with strong emotions such as panic, excitement, or anger. Individuals may get caught up in the collective emotion of the group, leading to actions that they might not take under different circumstances.

Simplification of Decision-Making:

Following the herd simplifies the decision-making process. In a world full of complexities and uncertainties, imitating the choices of others can serve as a heuristic, or mental shortcut, that makes decision-making easier and less stressful.

Ultimately, you've got to find your own cadence. You need to find out what you are good at and go and rally around that. The point is that we all have things we are good at. I can't do what you can do. Bill McDermott, the former CEO of SAP once said, "I do what I do well often. What I don't do well, I don't do at all." For instance, I may be a creative person and you may be more of an analytical person for all we know. And this determines what we can and cannot do in life and what we aspire to be.

However, human beings put value on certain things. For example, everyone wants their children to have a professional degree or want them to become doctors and engineers. They forget that we are not all the same. Maybe, your child is an artist or welder or tradesman.

We all need to look at the different designs and the theme around us. We can't all take the career path of Bill Gates or Steve Jobs, or even Elon Musk. Sure, we can take inspiration from them and try to aspire to be great, but we cannot be them. Dwelling excessively on emulating another person proves to be unproductive and necessitates a thorough self-reflection to identify and harness one's unique talents.

For example, I'm quite good at public speaking now, but when I first began to speak in public, I was quite mediocre. Now, I am actually pretty good at it, and in fact, I enjoy it thoroughly, but for me to have taken up a role where I had to do a lot of public speaking, I wasn't going to do very well. I did not like it and got a little nervous. Of course, I was not my best self and was underperforming. But I did find my best talents. Success in life often comes to down to have the guts to just get started. In a 2017 Harvard Commencement Address that Mark Zuckerberg gave, he said,

> *It's really good to be idealistic but be prepared to be misunderstood. Anyone working on a big vision is going to get called crazy even if you end up right.*

Anyone taking on a complex problem is going to get blamed for not full understanding it even though it's impossible to know everything up front. Anyone taking initiative will always get criticized for moving too fast because there's always someone who wants to slow you down. In our society, we're so afraid of making mistakes that we ignore the things wrong today if we do nothing. The reality is that anything we do today is going to have some issues in the future, but that can't stop us from getting started...

At some point, I was managing small teams and being respectful to them, and organizing when I was a young man, only 29 years old. I was practically running a big hospital, and most of the staff who were reporting to me were my parents' age. And so, it is really easy for young people to screw that up because you're stepping into such an authoritative position for the first time. People around you would have a lot to say, they would question your credibility, but you have to stand your ground. Even then, I would make it very clear that I was still very inexperienced, and there was a lot I did not know yet, but I learned as things progressed.

Supervising individuals who are significantly older, especially for a young person in a management position, presents unique challenges due to various factors related to experience, workplace dynamics, and social perceptions. Here are several reasons why this situation can be tough:

Perceived Lack of Experience:

Young managers may be perceived by older employees as lacking the necessary experience, both in terms of job-specific skills and life experience. This perception can lead to doubts about the young manager's competence and decisions, making it harder for them to gain respect and authority within the team.

Generational Differences:

Differences in values, communication styles, and work habits between generations can lead to misunderstandings and conflicts. Young managers might prioritize different work goals or employ different management styles than their older counterparts expect or are accustomed to, potentially causing friction.

Authority and Respect:

Earning respect can be particularly challenging for young managers overseeing older employees. In many cultures, age is associated with wisdom and experience, so older employees may struggle to accept authority from someone much younger than themselves. Building respect and credibility will often require additional effort from the young manager.

Insecurity and Intimidation:

Young managers may feel intimidated or insecure about supervising employees who have significantly more life and work experience. These feelings can undermine the manager's confidence and effectiveness in their role.

Resistance to Change:

Older employees might be more resistant to changes introduced by a younger manager, especially if these changes challenge long-standing processes or norms. This resistance may stem from a discomfort with the pace of change or a belief in the superiority of established methods.

Mentorship and Role Reversal:

Traditionally, mentorship flows from more experienced (often older) employees to less experienced (often younger) ones. When a young person manages older employees, this dynamic is reversed, which can be uncomfortable for both parties and complicate the establishment of productive mentor-mentee relationships.

Professional Development and Career Path Concerns:

Older employees may have concerns about their career progression and development opportunities under a younger manager. They might worry that a young manager will not adequately support their career goals or understand their professional aspirations.

Communication and Relatability:

Effective communication may be hindered by differences in preferences for communication technologies, jargon, or references. Young managers may use different methods or platforms for communication that older employees are less familiar with or comfortable using.

So, different designs are really about not being sabotaged by the path of somebody else but finding your own. The physiology of human beings is homogenous, sure, but we are all built different, and our strengths and weaknesses greatly vary. Always bear in mind the importance of pursuing your unique path, have confidence in your abilities, and recognize both your strengths and weaknesses.

Concentrating on tasks you excel at in the workplace and steering clear of those you struggle with mirrors the principle of division of labor, as outlined by Adam Smith in "The Wealth of Nations." Smith posited that dividing work into specific tasks and allowing individuals to specialize in what they are best at leads to increased efficiency and productivity. This specialization allows for a deeper mastery of skills, leading to superior quality of work and innovation. Just as Smith advocated for the economic benefits of this division in enhancing a nation's wealth, focusing on one's strengths within the workforce capitalizes on individual potential, optimizing overall team and organizational performance. In essence, by aligning personal proficiencies with specific roles, both the individual and the organization can achieve greater success and satisfaction, embodying the timeless wisdom of Smith's economic theories.

4

Adjusting Players

The most important aspect of success is a team that can collaborate well with each other. In a team, it is important that all the team players are on the same page. Building a strong organization is no different than building a strong army. Even in our own country's own history, there has been times where we have been cohesive and won decisively and times where we have been disjointed and suffered in defeat as a result.

It is always important to remember the wise words of someone when they said, "If I had 4 hours to cut down a tree, I'd spend 3 hours sharpening my axe." I have used this quote many times when discussing strategy in the as well as budgeting. It resonates the importance of being prepared and there is no better way to do that then having the best team on the field.

When you are developing a team, whether you're starting a project or just assessing the company's overall performance, having the right people is the strength it needs. To quote Steve Jobs again, "The secret of my success is that we have gone to exceptional lengths to hire the best people in the world."

The right players in the team should be the first and the foremost priority as they can determine the direction of your company. Building a team is not done overnight. It is, in fact, a lengthy process that takes a lot of careful decision-making. But how can you do your company the favor of building the best team? Well, how about you start with finding the best people, hiring the best people, and giving them the space to prove themselves. The most common mistake I see in young managers is that they micro-manage. There are seven reasons why this will hurt an organization:

Reduced Employee Autonomy:

Micromanagement limits employees' ability to make decisions and take initiative. This lack of autonomy can stifle creativity and innovation, as employees may feel they are not trusted to manage their tasks effectively.

Decreased Job Satisfaction:

Employees who are constantly monitored and given little freedom to exercise their judgment often experience lower job satisfaction. This dissatisfaction can lead to decreased motivation, engagement, and morale among the workforce.

Increased Stress:

Being under constant scrutiny can significantly increase stress levels among employees. High stress can impact mental and physical health, leading to burnout, higher absenteeism, and reduced productivity.

Inefficient Use of Time:

Micromanagers spend a considerable amount of time overseeing minute details of their employees' work, rather than focusing on strategic planning and higher-level tasks. This can lead to inefficiencies and missed opportunities for the organization.

Impeded Personal and Professional Development:

When employees are not given the chance to work independently, solve problems, and make decisions, their personal and professional growth is hindered. Over time, this can result in a workforce that is less skilled and less adaptable to change.

Deterioration of Trust:

Micromanagement undermines trust between managers and their teams. Employees may feel their abilities and contributions are undervalued, damaging the relationship with their manager and the organization as a whole.

Increased Turnover:

The negative effects of micromanagement on job satisfaction, stress, and professional growth can lead to higher turnover rates. Replacing employees is costly and can disrupt the continuity and cohesion of teams.

Why were George Washington, Abraham Lincoln, and FDR ranked as the top three presidents of all time? They delegated effectively to their subordinates; in effect they lived out the words of yet another Steve Jobs quote when he said, "It doesn't make sense to hire smart people and then tell them what to. We hire smart people so they can tell us what to do."

George Washington's ability to delegate power and responsibility effectively, particularly to Alexander Hamilton, was a cornerstone of his success as both a military leader during the Revolutionary War and later as the first President of the United States. This strategic delegation showcased Washington's leadership prowess and foresight in recognizing and utilizing the talents of those around him for the greater good.

Abraham Lincoln, who looked up to Washington, said this when describing him:

Washington is the mightiest name of earth – long since mightiest in the cause of civil liberty, still mightiest in moral reformation. On that name no eulogy is expected. It cannot be. To add brightness to the sun or glory to the name of Washington is alike impossible. Let none attempt it. In solemn awe pronounce his name, and in its naked deathless splendor leave it shining on.

Humility is so important in leadership because without it, you can't attack problems with the right amount of velocity. To be humble means that you're secure with yourself. When you're around a secure person, there's a different feeling to your interaction with them. They are not trying to impress or force their opinion on you. In short, you find more security in your own self because of their security in themselves. Another example of Washington being secure with himself is when he rejected the crown.

When you think of the head of an organization, you typically think of someone who is power hungry and looking to advance their own interest, right? But with Washington that wasn't the case and when we look at Lincoln, we will see that is not case either.

He also knew that he to delegate serious power to lead effectively. His presidency during the American Civil War is a prime example of effective leadership through strategic delegation, particularly in his relationship with Generals Ulysses S. Grant and William Tecumseh Sherman. Lincoln's ability to entrust significant responsibilities to these military leaders was crucial in turning the tide of the war in favor of the Union and solidifying his success as a wartime president.

Delegating to Ulysses S. Grant:

Lincoln's delegation to Grant began in earnest after Grant's victories at Fort Henry and Fort Donelson. Recognizing Grant's determination and effectiveness, Lincoln promoted him to Lieutenant General in 1864, giving him command of all Union armies. Lincoln provided Grant with the autonomy to devise and execute military strategies, understanding that Grant's aggressive approach could decisively end the war. This trust was not misplaced; Grant's Overland Campaign and his siege of Petersburg were critical in weakening Confederate forces and eventually leading to the surrender of Robert E. Lee at Appomattox Court House.

Impact of Delegation

Lincoln's delegation to Grant and Sherman had several key impacts:

Strategic Initiative:

By empowering Grant and Sherman, Lincoln ensured that the Union took the strategic initiative, shifting the war's momentum in favor of the North.

Morale:

The successes achieved under Grant and Sherman's leadership boosted the morale of the Union, both on the battlefield and at home.

Unified Vision:

Lincoln, Grant, and Sherman shared a unified vision for the war's end—preserving the Union and ending slavery. This shared goal ensured cohesive action despite the delegation of authority.

Political Success:

The military victories achieved under Grant and Sherman's command were crucial for Lincoln's re-election in 1864, allowing him to continue his leadership and see the war to its conclusion.

Lincoln's successful delegation was rooted in his leadership qualities: his ability to recognize talent, his willingness to trust his generals' judgment, and his strategic foresight. By delegating significant power to Grant and Sherman, Lincoln not only facilitated key military victories but also demonstrated the strength of his leadership during one of the most challenging periods in American history. This approach highlights the importance of choosing the right leaders, trusting them to execute their roles, and the transformative power of effective delegation in achieving overarching objectives.

Following in Lincoln's footsteps, FDR knew that he had to effectively delegate to be successful in World War 2. The person who he trusted the most was General George Marshall. This delegation was instrumental in the successful execution of the war strategy and contributed to FDR's effectiveness and success as a wartime president.

The Delegation to George C. Marshall

FDR recognized Marshall's exceptional organizational and strategic planning skills early on. Upon appointing Marshall in 1939, Roosevelt empowered him with wide-ranging authority over the U.S. Army's expansion and modernization, which was crucial as the nation prepared for the likelihood of entering World War II. Marshall's role involved not only military preparedness and strategy but also significant input into key policy decisions. In May of 1940, at about a year, George Marshall needed $50 billion for the military, but FDR had talked about cutting the military budget, in part because he was about to be running for his third term and wanted to position himself well to voters. Can you imagine not trying to tell your boss that he or she is dead wrong? Don't you think it would be even harder if he/she was the president of the United States? Marshall was smart enough to seek out the advice of Henry Morgenthau Jr., who was a long-time friend of the president. Morgenthau told Marshall that when they went to see the president, "stand right up and tell him what you think … There are few people who do it and he likes it." I've found in my career that listening to others is not passive as many people think; instead, it is the most powerful action you can take. Truly being open to guidance doesn't mean that you don't know the answer, it means you are humble enough to admit that there's a possibility, as slight as it could be, that you don't know the answer. Having that type of mentality is the only way to grow, because you only grow when you are tested, and in order to pass a test, you must listen.

Key Aspects and Outcomes of This Delegation:
Strategic Leadership:

Marshall was instrumental in developing and overseeing the execution of comprehensive military strategies, including the planning and execution of major operations in both the European and Pacific theaters. His oversight helped ensure that the Allied forces remained coordinated and focused on common objectives.

Global Coalition Building:

Marshall played a pivotal role in building and maintaining the Allied coalition, working closely with political and military leaders from other nations. This was essential for the cooperative effort needed to defeat the Axis powers. Roosevelt's trust in Marshall allowed for effective U.S. leadership on the global stage, facilitating strategies like the "Europe First" approach.

Rapid Army Expansion:

Under Marshall's guidance, the U.S. Army underwent one of the most rapid expansions in history, growing from a modest, poorly equipped force into a formidable, world-leading military power. This expansion was critical for the U.S. to assume its role in the Allied victory.

Innovation in Warfare:

Marshall supported innovations in warfare, including the development and use of new technologies and strategies. His openness to new ideas contributed to the Allied forces' tactical advantage.

Implementation of the G.I. Bill:

Marshall also advocated for the G.I. Bill, understanding the importance of taking care of soldiers returning from war. This legislation, supported by Roosevelt, provided veterans with benefits that helped them reintegrate into civilian life, furthering education and spurring post-war economic growth.

Impact of Roosevelt's Delegation to Marshall

FDR's delegation to Marshall allowed for a more effective and efficient war effort, as it capitalized on Marshall's expertise in military strategy and personnel management. It also allowed Roosevelt to focus on the broader aspects of wartime leadership, including economic mobilization, coalition building, and the home front's morale. This division of responsibility was a key factor in the Allies' eventual victory and highlighted the importance of trust and strategic delegation in leadership.

By entrusting Marshall with significant military leadership responsibilities, FDR demonstrated a keen understanding of his own strengths and limitations, as well as a profound trust in the capabilities of those around him. This approach not only facilitated a successful wartime strategy but also solidified FDR's legacy as a leader capable of navigating the complexities of global conflict through effective delegation.

And while you are at it, look beyond people's race, ethnicities, and backgrounds. After all, Desmond Tutu once said, ""A person is a person through other persons." It is because talent and skill are something one acquires and has nothing to do with who a person is or where they belong. You should not care if someone is black, or brown, or yellow. Incorporating individuals from diverse backgrounds into a business enriches the organization with a mosaic of perspectives, driving innovation and creativity by merging distinct ideas and problem-solving approaches. This diversity fosters a more dynamic workplace culture, enhancing team collaboration and understanding by exposing employees to a variety of viewpoints and experiences. Moreover, it positions the business to better understand and cater to a global customer base, ultimately improving customer satisfaction and expanding market reach.

As a business owner, you must have an eye for the best candidates. Some prominent traits to be found in them are reliability, conscientiousness, consistency, and hard work. They are going to treat your company like their own, take the initiative, and know how to make it work as a team. I not only like to go to Chick-Fil-a to eat their delicious chicken sandwiches, but through the years I have learned much about the tremendous leadership that founder Truett Cathy possessed. I'll boil down what he did in a few points below:

Innovation in Product and Service:

Cathy was the inventor of the chicken sandwich, a simple yet revolutionary idea that set the foundation for Chick-fil-A's menu and distinguished it from competitors. This innovation, coupled with a focus on high-quality ingredients and preparation methods, helped establish Chick-fil-A as a leader in the fast-food industry.

Customer Service Excellence:

Truett Cathy placed a high priority on exceptional customer service, adopting the policy of responding with "my pleasure" to customers' thanks, which became a hallmark of Chick-fil-A's customer service. This attention to making each customer feel valued and respected contributed significantly to building a loyal customer base.

Strong Core Values and Corporate Culture:

Cathy was deeply religious and integrated his Christian beliefs into his business practices. This included keeping Chick-fil-A locations closed on Sundays to allow employees a day of rest and worship, which was both a reflection of his values and a unique aspect of the company's operational model. His commitment to family values, integrity, and generosity helped shape a strong corporate culture that attracted employees and customers alike.

Investment in People:

Cathy believed in investing in people, whether it was through scholarship programs for employees, creating a family-oriented work environment, or his involvement in philanthropic efforts aimed at supporting youth and education. By treating employees well and providing opportunities for growth, he ensured a motivated and dedicated workforce.

Cathy knew that the most successful employees do not shy away from working hard and are always up to face many challenges without flinching. These people are the true team players, and they are going to be the people that are the learners.

They crave recognition and want to make a change in this world. What adjusting your players really means is to build the best team, send them off to the playing field, and let them do their magic! Artists, the most compelling and the most captivating people, should make it to your team. Similarly, personality A leaders, empaths, and so many more traits that you can combine to send your best to elevate your company's success.

In a business, people with Type A personalities are like superheroes. They work super hard and pay attention to every little detail to make sure everything goes perfectly. They have a lot of energy and never give up, which helps them solve big problems and reach their goals. Having someone like this on a team is great because they lead by example and keep everyone moving forward, making sure the business does its very best.

My company, which is not a big company by its size in any way, has no specific training program. In companies like mine, the work one does and all the learning that follows come with exploring your role and touching upon other avenues. If you need proper training, then you can work for bigger companies. This is because newly established companies are still in their trial-and-error phase, and they don't know what exactly works for them just yet. If you are someone who could do successful experimenting, then you may be the right fit for a smaller and relatively newer setup because these are the companies that are actually adjusting players in the field. They never know which combination works best for them.

Some people prefer working for larger companies due to the stability and structure they offer. Big companies often provide comprehensive benefits, such as health insurance and retirement plans, which can be very attractive. There's also the chance to work on large-scale projects that can make a significant impact, offering a sense of pride and accomplishment. Furthermore, bigger organizations typically offer more opportunities for career advancement, allowing individuals to climb the professional ladder within the same company.

On the other hand, working for smaller companies appeals to those who cherish flexibility and a close-knit community feel. In a smaller setting, employees can enjoy a greater sense of involvement in the company's direction and decisions, fostering a deeper personal connection to their work. These environments often allow for more rapid professional growth due to the diverse range of tasks and responsibilities one might take on. Additionally, smaller companies can provide a more relaxed atmosphere, with less bureaucracy, making it easier for innovative ideas to be heard and implemented.

5

Moving The Price

This is one of my favorite concepts and is the most relevant to the CEOs and executives of the publicly listed companies whose stocks are trading on the stock market. So, you see how the stock price is a metric to judge the company's performance and to use as an indicator of how much competence the company has. Warren Buffett might have put it best when he said that, *"The stock market is designed to transfer money from the Active to the Patient."*

It shows a company's internal controls and how robust its policies and procedures are to ensure that its operations are being run smoothly. It is also a reflection of how compliant a company is to the regulatory authority and is also a good indicator of a company's financial health.

There are so many professional analysts out there who are closely monitoring the stock prices of companies that interest them, and so one can say that, in a way, a company's stock price becomes crucial to a company's image. The direction of a stock price is also closely tied to the performance of the company. So, if the stock price is going up, it is usually seen as a good sign for the company, and if it goes down, it is taken as a red flag for the company's performance.

As a CEO, the stock price is what you worry about primarily. As a CEO, every day you wake up, moving the price naturally becomes the first thing you worry about. I have been doing this for about the last 12 years, and I'm struggling with a lot of decisions that I can make. Do I work on this or work on that? Do I call this person or not? What is my priority list for that day or for the month? And what can I do that is going to move that price in my favor? What is it that I can do that is going to have an impact on my company's image and make that stock price stable?

There are a million different things I can choose to do as a CEO. I mean, I can choose to go fishing, in which the stock price is probably not going to do well. Or, I can choose to go and take someone to dinner or figure out another analysis where we can make more money that day. If you are an entrepreneur or an individual, or even if you're an employee, you'd think, "What can I do today to move that stock price up?"

And "moving the price" is one concept that dictates your to-do list. It helps prioritize the things that matter most to your company and reflects well on your decision-making abilities as an executive. It so happens that there are so many people around you and so many tensions in the world that take your focus away from the things that are important.

If you want to stand out as an employee, then you know, doing small desk-related tasks will not get you noticed. Just like the executives, pulling off strategies that are actually going to "move the price" up is what really matters at the end of the day. It is what will get you the promotion you need.

While mainstream factors like earnings reports, market trends, and industry performance are commonly watched indicators for stock price movements, several often overlooked factors can also significantly influence a stock's price. Here are four or five such factors:

Changes in Management:

Shifts in a company's leadership can have a profound impact on investor confidence and, consequently, stock prices. A new CEO or management team with a strong track record can lead to positive market reactions, as investors anticipate improved performance and strategic decisions.

Regulatory Changes:

Changes in government regulations or policies that affect a specific industry can influence stock prices. For example, new environmental regulations might benefit renewable energy companies but could be costly for traditional energy firms, affecting their stock prices differently.

Short Interest:

The level of short interest in a stock, or the number of shares that have been sold short but not yet covered, can be an indicator of market sentiment. A high short interest may lead to a short squeeze, where short sellers rush to buy back shares to cover their positions, driving the stock price up.

Institutional Ownership Changes:

The buying and selling activities of institutional investors, like mutual funds and pension funds, can significantly impact stock prices. These large trades can signal confidence or lack thereof in a company, influencing other investors' perceptions and actions.

Currency Fluctuations: For companies that operate internationally, changes in currency exchange rates can affect earnings and profits when converted back to the company's home currency. A weakening domestic currency can lead to higher reported earnings for companies with significant overseas operations, potentially boosting the stock price.

Even if your hospital is not listed on the stock market, there are several things that a hospital executive can do to help grow the company. Here they are below:

Expanding Services and Specialties:

By adding new medical services or specialties, a hospital can attract more patients, including those seeking specialized care that may not be available elsewhere in the area. This could include introducing cutting-edge medical technologies, opening new departments (like geriatrics or telemedicine), or enhancing existing ones (such as cardiology or oncology).

Improving Patient Experience:

Focusing on patient satisfaction can lead to higher retention rates, more referrals, and a better reputation. Administrators can invest in training staff for better patient interactions, upgrading facilities for comfort, and implementing efficient patient flow management systems to reduce wait times.

Strategic Partnerships and Alliances:

Forming partnerships with other healthcare providers, such as clinics, rehabilitation centers, or specialized medical practices, can expand the hospital's network and provide integrated care solutions. Collaborations with academic institutions for research and training can also enhance the hospital's standing in the medical community.

Enhancing Digital Presence and Telehealth Services:

Developing a robust digital presence through a user-friendly website, active social media engagement, and online patient portals can improve accessibility and patient engagement. Expanding telehealth services caters to a broader patient base, especially in underserved areas, and responds to the increasing demand for remote healthcare.

Focusing on High-Quality Care and Accreditations:

Achieving and maintaining high standards of care, as evidenced by accreditations from recognized healthcare organizations, can distinguish a hospital from its competitors. Continuous quality improvement initiatives and excellence in patient care can attract more patients and healthcare professionals.

Community Outreach and Health Education:

Engaging with the local community through health education programs, free clinics, or wellness events can raise the hospital's profile and build trust within the community. This approach can turn the hospital into a go-to resource for health-related issues, thereby growing its patient base.

Optimizing Operational Efficiency:

Streamlining operations to reduce waste and improve efficiency can lower costs and improve the patient experience. This might involve adopting new technologies for patient management, improving supply chain logistics, or reevaluating service contracts to ensure competitive pricing.

As a hospital executive, you have the unique opportunity to catalyze revenue growth by embracing innovative healthcare solutions and expanding the range of specialized services offered, thus attracting a broader patient base. By investing in state-of-the-art medical technology and fostering a culture of excellence in patient care, you can significantly enhance patient satisfaction, leading to higher retention rates and positive word-of-mouth referrals. Strategic partnerships with other healthcare providers and community outreach programs can further elevate your hospital's profile, drawing in more patients seeking quality care. Remember, your visionary leadership and commitment to excellence are key drivers in propelling your hospital towards financial success and community well-being.

6

Managing Revenue Vs. Expenses

This is probably the most important aspect of running a business. I am going to throw out some things that I think will be enlightening for some folks. In other words, when you look at an accounting ledger, there is a column on the left for revenues and a column on the right for expenses. So, I maintain that the effort should always go on to the revenue side of that ledger.

What do I mean by that? Well, what I mean is that about 90% of your efforts need to be focused on the revenue side. It means that money coming into the company could be any amount, maybe even just 10%, but still needs to weigh more. Here are some reasons why it is so important to put a lot of emphasis on the revenue side:

Sustainability and Growth:

Revenue is the lifeblood of any business, providing the necessary funds to cover operational costs, pay salaries, and invest in growth opportunities. Without adequate revenue, a business cannot sustain its operations nor can it plan for future expansion or improvement.

Attracting Investment:

A strong revenue stream demonstrates market demand and business viability, making the company more attractive to potential investors and lenders. Investors typically look for businesses with growing revenues as they indicate a successful business model and the potential for high returns on their investments.

Building Credibility and Reputation:

Consistently high revenue figures can enhance a business's credibility in its industry and with stakeholders, including suppliers, customers, and potential partners. This credibility can open up new opportunities, such as favorable credit terms with suppliers or strategic partnerships with other companies.

Risk Management:

A healthy revenue stream provides a buffer against market fluctuations, economic downturns, or unexpected costs. This financial cushion allows businesses to navigate tough times without resorting to drastic measures like significant layoffs or shutting down operations.

Reinvestment Opportunities:

Lastly, generating significant revenue gives a business the opportunity to reinvest in itself—be it through research and development, marketing efforts, new technology, or expanding the workforce. This reinvestment is crucial for innovation, improving competitive advantage, and ensuring long-term success.

Here is a bit more about that. Revenue is an important aspect because I can affect revenue by making simple tweaks. However, this is not true for incurring expenses. On the expense side, there is very little that you can do, and there are always certain and fixed things that must be entered. It is rather straightforward; you have got to pay your utility bills; you've got to pay your car allowances, mortgage, or any other expenses.

I might be able to move those numbers a little tiny bit. But it is just not an area where I'm interested in spending a lot of time. And, you know, I know I will talk to people who are proud of saving $10 on their cable bill this week because it is interesting and kind of an impossible task to do. And, I will advise them that why don't they go and make $100 instead.

You know, instead of worrying about that, I should focus on something that I have control over because expenses will get fixed eventually. Again, I do not want to appear arrogant when I say this, but I'm just saying that as you walk through developing your career or your own company, work on the revenues. There are absolutely no caps on that.

You can make a thousand bucks, or you can make a million a month. It does not matter. As for your expenses, I have already mentioned that you cannot move as much as. So, if I am holding up a muscle, I'm putting 90% of that into revenue and only 10% of that through expense control.

Focusing solely on controlling expenses, while important for maintaining a healthy bottom line, can be detrimental to a business's long-term success and growth for several reasons:

Stifles Growth and Innovation:

Excessive cost-cutting measures can restrict a company's ability to invest in new technologies, research and development, and market expansion efforts. This lack of investment in innovation and growth can leave the business trailing behind competitors who are more willing to allocate resources towards future development.

Deteriorates Product and Service Quality:

Extreme cost-cutting often leads to compromises in the quality of products and services offered. This can result in customer dissatisfaction and erosion of brand loyalty, ultimately impacting revenue as customers turn to competitors for superior offerings.

Undermines Employee Morale and Productivity:

A singular focus on reducing expenses can lead to workforce reductions, cuts in employee benefits, and insufficient resources for employees to perform their jobs effectively. Such measures can demoralize employees, reduce productivity, and increase turnover rates, further affecting the business's operational efficiency and reputation.

Hampers Competitive Advantage:

Businesses that concentrate only on minimizing expenses may miss out on opportunities to build a strong competitive advantage through differentiation, such as offering exceptional customer service or unique product features. A failure to differentiate can make a business more vulnerable to price competition and reduce its ability to command premium pricing.

Short-Term Gains vs. Long-Term Sustainability:

While controlling expenses can lead to immediate improvements in profitability, it is a strategy that prioritizes short-term gains over long-term sustainability. Without a balanced focus on revenue growth and strategic investment, businesses risk stagnation and may struggle to adapt to changing market conditions, ultimately jeopardizing their long-term viability.

To conclude, focusing on growing revenue opens the door to limitless possibilities for a company, fueling not just survival but thriving innovation and expansion. By channelling energy into enhancing products, services, and customer experiences, you lay the foundation for a resilient and dynamic business that attracts more customers and establishes a strong market presence. Revenue growth fosters an environment ripe for investment in new technologies and talent, driving further innovation and competitive advantage. Remember, while cost-cutting can provide short-term relief, it is the pursuit of revenue growth that paints the future of a company in bright, bold colors, promising sustainability and success.

7

Financial Statements

I've found that just hearing the term *financial statements* can intimidate people. If you understand how they work; however, you cannot only stand them, but start to use them to your benefit.

Here are some bullet points on how to use financial statements in hospitals:

Decision Making:

Management uses financial statements to make critical decisions regarding expansion, budget allocations, and resource management. For example, analyzing the profitability of different departments can guide decisions about where to invest in new medical technologies or services.

Financial Health Assessment:

Assessing financial health involves evaluating the balance between revenue (from patient services, insurance payments, etc.) and expenses (such as salaries, medical supplies, and operational costs). This assessment helps stakeholders understand if the hospital can sustain its operations, invest in new equipment, or expand its services.

Performance Evaluation:

Financial statements allow for the evaluation of a hospital's financial performance over time, including its ability to generate income from its operations, manage its costs effectively, and maintain cash flow to support ongoing and future needs. Comparing performance across periods can help identify trends, such as an increase in patient volume or changes in reimbursement rates from insurance companies.

Regulatory Compliance:

Speciality healthcare facilities, especially those that are publicly funded or non-profit, must adhere to specific financial reporting standards and regulations. Financial statements ensure compliance with these requirements, helping to maintain eligibility for government funding, grants, and charitable contributions.

Strategic Planning:

Financial statements are critical for strategic planning. They help in setting realistic financial goals, preparing budgets, and forecasting future financial needs. This planning might include expanding into new services, upgrading facilities, or implementing cost-saving measures to improve efficiency.

Credit Assessment:

When hospitals seek financing for new projects or equipment, lenders use the hospital's financial statements to assess its ability to repay loans. A strong financial position can lead to better loan terms and interest rates, reducing the cost of borrowing.

Investor Confidence:

For entities that rely on investors or philanthropy, transparent and regular financial reporting can build confidence among potential and current backers. This transparency assures them that their investments are being managed wisely and contributing to the hospital's growth and service improvement.

Taxation:

Although many hospitals operate as non-profit entities and may be exempt from certain taxes, they must still file financial statements with tax authorities to maintain their tax-exempt status. These statements are used to ensure that the hospital complies with tax laws and regulations, including reporting on sources of income and expenditures.

In each of these areas, the specific challenges and operations of a hospital—such as the complexity of healthcare billing, the critical nature of its services, and the importance of maintaining high-quality patient care—are reflected in how its financial statements are interpreted and used. The ultimate goal of these financial analyses is to ensure that the hospital can continue to provide essential healthcare services to the community it serves, while also maintaining financial sustainability and compliance with regulatory standards.

Through the years, I've seen the following mistakes when people are analyzing financial statements.

Overlooking Context and Industry Standards:

Comparing financial metrics without considering the context of the industry or economic environment can lead to incorrect conclusions. Different industries have varying financial norms and practices, and economic conditions can greatly affect financial performance.

Ignoring Non-Financial Factors:

Focusing solely on the numbers without considering non-financial factors such as market trends, regulatory changes, or the competitive landscape can lead to an incomplete analysis. These factors can significantly impact future performance.

Failing to Consider Accounting Policies:

Different companies may use different accounting policies and practices, which can affect how financial statements are presented. Failing to adjust for these differences can mislead comparative analysis, especially when looking at companies across borders or industries.

Relying Too Much on Historical Data:

While historical data is essential for understanding past performance, it may not always be a reliable predictor of future success. Overreliance on past performance without considering future growth drivers or challenges can be misleading.

Misinterpreting Ratios:

Financial ratios are a key tool in analyzing financial statements, but misinterpreting what these ratios indicate can lead to incorrect conclusions. Understanding what each ratio measures and its limitations is crucial.

Neglecting the Footnotes:

The footnotes in financial statements can contain critical information about accounting policies, potential liabilities, and other factors that can materially impact the understanding of a company's financial health. Ignoring these details can result in an incomplete analysis.

Focusing Solely on Short-Term Results:

Short-term financial performance is important, but it's also necessary to consider long-term trends and sustainability. Focusing too narrowly on short-term results can miss the bigger picture of a company's overall health and strategy.

Confirmation Bias:

Analysts may fall into the trap of seeking out information that confirms their preexisting beliefs or hypotheses about a company, while ignoring evidence that contradicts them. This bias can lead to flawed analyses and decisions.

Overemphasis on Profitability:

While profitability is a key indicator of financial health, focusing exclusively on profits without considering cash flow, debt levels, and other financial metrics can provide a misleading picture of a company's financial stability.

Not Reviewing Adjusted Financials:

Companies often present adjusted financials to provide a clearer picture of ongoing operations by excluding one-time items or non-operational expenses. However, analysts must carefully consider these adjustments to ensure they are reasonable and not designed to overly inflate performance metrics.

A good knowledge of financial statements is crucial for a company's success for several reasons. First, it empowers company leaders to make well-informed decisions about investments, cost management, and strategic planning, directly contributing to optimizing the company's financial performance and growth potential. Additionally, understanding financial statements helps in monitoring and managing the company's financial health, ensuring sustainability by identifying financial strengths and weaknesses early. This enables timely interventions to mitigate risks and capitalize on opportunities. Furthermore, proficient management and presentation of financial statements can significantly enhance stakeholder confidence, attracting investors, lenders, and partners by demonstrating financial transparency and accountability. This, in turn, can lead to better financing terms, increased investment, and stronger business relationships, all of which are vital components of a successful company.

8

Targets vs. Budgets

In a hospital setting, targets and budgets play a critical role in ensuring efficient, effective, and sustainable healthcare delivery. Here are some points highlighting their importance:

Resource Allocation:

Hospitals have limited resources, including staff, equipment, and funds. Budgets help allocate these resources efficiently, ensuring that high-priority areas, such as emergency services or critical care units, receive adequate funding to meet patient needs effectively.

Cost Control:

With rising healthcare costs, hospitals face the challenge of providing high-quality care while managing expenses. Budgets set spending limits and help identify areas where costs can be reduced without compromising patient care, such as through bulk purchasing of supplies or investing in energy-efficient technologies.

Financial Health and Sustainability:

Budgets are essential for maintaining the financial health of a hospital. They ensure that the hospital lives within its means, generating enough revenue to cover expenses and invest in future growth. This financial stability is crucial for the long-term sustainability of healthcare services.

Performance Monitoring:

Targets and budgets are benchmarks for performance. By setting specific financial and operational targets, hospitals can monitor progress and performance over time. This helps in identifying areas of success and areas needing improvement, facilitating continuous quality improvement in patient care and operational efficiency.

Strategic Planning:

Targets and budgets are integral to strategic planning. They translate the hospital's long-term goals into actionable plans and financial forecasts, helping to steer the hospital towards its vision. For instance, if a hospital aims to expand its services, budgets would include allocations for new facilities, equipment, and staff.

Stakeholder Accountability:

Hospitals often answer to various stakeholders, including government bodies, donors, and the community. Targets and budgets provide a transparent framework for reporting on how resources are being used, ensuring accountability and building trust among stakeholders.

Regulatory Compliance:

In many regions, hospitals must meet specific financial management standards and regulations. Budgets help ensure compliance with these requirements, avoiding legal or financial penalties and contributing to the overall integrity of the healthcare system.

Encourages Innovation:

By setting targets for cost-saving and efficiency improvements, hospitals can encourage innovation within their staff. This could lead to the development of new, more efficient treatment methods, or the adoption of cutting-edge technology that improves patient care and operational effectiveness.

As we close this chapter on the pivotal role of targets versus budgets within the hospital system, it becomes clear that these mechanisms are not just administrative tools but the very heartbeat of healthcare management. Targets articulate the aspirations of a hospital, setting a course towards excellence in patient care and operational efficiency, while budgets provide the tangible framework to turn these aspirations into reality, ensuring resources are allocated wisely and sustainably. Together, they create a dynamic interplay that propels a hospital forward, balancing the scales of financial prudence with the uncompromising commitment to saving lives and fostering well-being. In essence, the judicious crafting and careful execution of targets and budgets are what enable a hospital system to navigate the complexities of healthcare delivery, ensuring it remains a beacon of hope and healing in the community it serves.

9

Strategy

As the healthcare executive, it is my privilege to steer our ship through the ever-evolving healthcare landscape, guided by our strategic business plan. Our mission is not just to heal but to innovate, inspire, and uplift, ensuring that we not only meet the present needs of our community but also anticipate the future's demands.

Vision and Execution: The Foundation of Success

"Vision without action is merely a dream. Action without vision just passes the time. Vision with action can change the world." – Joel A. Barker

This quote beautifully encapsulates our journey. Like a skilled quarterback leading a football team to a Super Bowl victory, we must combine foresight with precision execution. Consider the historic 1969 Super Bowl III, where Joe Namath of the New York Jets led his team to an unexpected victory by not only having the vision of winning but also executing his plays flawlessly against the Baltimore Colts. Similarly, our hospital's strategic plan is our playbook, with each department and team member playing a critical role in executing our vision.

Innovation and Adaptability: Learning from the Greats

Innovation and adaptability are at the heart of our strategy. We draw inspiration from the likes of Steve Jobs, who once said, "Innovation distinguishes between a leader and a follower." In the realm of American sports, this mirrors the innovative "West Coast Offense" in football, a strategy that changed the game with its focus on passing instead of running. Just as this offense revolutionized football, our hospital is committed to pioneering medical innovations that revolutionize healthcare delivery.

Teamwork and Collaboration: The Spirit of Unity:

"The whole is greater than the sum of its parts." – Aristotle

Nowhere is this truer than within the walls of a hospital. The 1980 U.S. Olympic hockey team's "Miracle on Ice" serves as a powerful reminder of what can be achieved when a group of individuals comes together with a common purpose. Each department, from surgeons to administrative staff, plays an integral part in our collective success. By fostering a culture of collaboration and respect, we can overcome any challenge.

Resilience and Perseverance: The Path to Excellence:

"Success is not final, failure is not fatal: It is the courage to continue that counts." – Unknown author

The healthcare industry is fraught with challenges, from regulatory hurdles to the unpredictable nature of patient care. Yet, like Michael Jordan, who was cut from his high school basketball team only to become one of the greatest athletes of all time, we must embrace failure as a stepping stone to success. Our ability to persevere through adversity is what will define our legacy.

Community and Compassion: Beyond the Walls of Our Hospital{

"To know even one life has breathed easier because you have lived. This is to have succeeded." – Ralph Waldo Emerson

Our responsibility extends beyond providing medical care; it encompasses improving the overall well-being of our community. Just as a sports team can unite a city, a hospital has the power to heal and inspire our community. Through outreach programs, educational initiatives, and compassionate care, we can make a lasting impact on the lives of those we serve.

A Beacon of Hope and Healing:

As we forge ahead, guided by our strategic business plan, let us remember that our journey is about more than just achieving financial targets or meeting performance metrics. It's about changing lives, advancing medical science, and leaving a legacy of hope and healing.

In the words of Socrates, "The secret of change is to focus all of your energy not on fighting the old, but on building the new." Together, as a unified team driven by passion and purpose, we will build a brighter future for our hospital and the communities we serve.

10

Think You Can Handle Healthcare?

The healthcare world is vast and getting more specialized every day. I was trained in Hospital Administration which arguably is the most complex entity in the healthcare space.

Hospital administration is often considered the most complex entity in the healthcare space due to a myriad of factors that require careful coordination, strategic planning, and adept management. Here are several reasons why this is the case:

Multifaceted Operations:

Hospitals are multifunctional entities that combine aspects of healthcare delivery, teaching, research, and sometimes community services. This requires administrators to oversee not just medical services, but also education and training programs, research initiatives, and outreach efforts, each with its own set of challenges and requirements.

Diverse Stakeholders:

Hospital administrators must navigate the needs and expectations of a wide range of stakeholders, including patients, medical and non-medical staff, insurance companies, regulatory bodies, and the community at large. Balancing these interests, especially when they conflict, requires nuanced decision-making and diplomacy.

Regulatory Compliance:

The healthcare industry is one of the most heavily regulated sectors. Hospitals must comply with a complex web of laws and regulations at the local, state, and federal levels, covering everything from patient privacy and safety to billing practices and environmental standards. Ensuring compliance requires extensive knowledge of the regulatory landscape and constant vigilance.

Financial Management:

Hospitals operate in a financially challenging environment, with pressure to manage costs while maintaining high standards of care. This involves intricate budgeting, negotiation with insurers and suppliers, management of billing and reimbursement processes, and investment in technologies and facilities. Financial sustainability is crucial, yet often difficult to achieve.

Technological Advancements:

Keeping pace with rapid technological changes in healthcare, from electronic health records (EHRs) to cutting-edge medical equipment, presents another layer of complexity. Administrators must make informed decisions about which technologies to invest in, how to implement them, and how to train staff, all while ensuring that these advancements improve care quality and efficiency.

Quality and Safety:

Ensuring the highest standards of patient care and safety is a core responsibility. This requires implementing and monitoring quality control measures, accreditation standards, and patient satisfaction initiatives. The complexity of healthcare services, coupled with the inherent risks of medical treatments, makes this a particularly challenging aspect of hospital administration.

Human Resource Management:

Hospitals are labor-intensive organizations with a diverse workforce that includes highly skilled professionals such as doctors and nurses, as well as support staff, technicians, and administrative personnel. Recruiting, training, and retaining a motivated workforce in a competitive and often stressful environment requires sophisticated HR management strategies.

Crisis Management and Emergency Preparedness: Hospitals must be prepared to respond to emergencies, ranging from natural disasters to pandemics and mass casualty events. This requires detailed planning, resource allocation, and the ability to adapt quickly to rapidly changing circumstances.

In summary, the complexity of hospital administration stems from the need to juggle multiple operational, financial, regulatory, and clinical factors, all within a framework that demands both high efficiency and uncompromising standards of care. The role requires a blend of expertise in healthcare, business management, and leadership, making it a uniquely challenging position within the healthcare sector.

The variety of skill sets from that have to be managed is broad. Each piece of the personnel puzzle have to be taken care of from dietary and housekeeping to Neurology and other complex sciences and specialist. All are apart of the orchestra and irreplaceable to operate a high performing and regulatory compliant hospital.

In a hospital, the intricate interaction between various departments mirrors the coordinated effort required in an orchestra to perform a symphony. Each department, from emergency services and surgery to radiology and pharmacy, plays a distinct role, akin to different musical sections such as strings, brass, woodwinds, and percussion. Just as a conductor leads an orchestra, ensuring that all sections come in at the right times and harmonize with each other, hospital administration oversees the integration of all departments. This coordination ensures that patient care is seamless, with each department contributing its expertise at the right moment, much like musicians contributing their unique sounds to create a harmonious piece.

Communication channels between departments act like the musical scores that guide each musician's performance, ensuring that everyone is on the same page. For instance, the patient care process might begin in the emergency department, move to imaging for diagnosis, proceed to surgery if needed, and then to recovery and rehabilitation, requiring a smooth handoff at each stage. Technology plays a role similar to that of an orchestral score's annotations, providing real-time updates and patient information to every department involved in the care process. Through this orchestrated effort, hospitals achieve the ultimate goal of providing comprehensive, high-quality care, just as an orchestra strives to deliver a flawless performance of a symphony.

There are several keys to success that I have seen in exceptional executives in healthcare. Working in tandem with clinical staff evaluating equipment and service expansion it vital. There was always a tendency for physicians particularly specialist to endorse capital expenditures that give them a professional edge to offer their patients. Offering state of the art services can elevate their patient base and allow them to market them to expand their practice. This is where the evaluation of these expenditures have to be scrutinized by executives before making the investment. The temptation for zealous sales folks to threw out a lot of spin that you have to carefully examine.

Capital expenditures in a hospital setting are subject to heavy scrutiny by administrators for several critical reasons. First, these investments often represent significant financial commitments that can impact the hospital's budget and financial health for years to come. Hospitals operate within tight financial constraints, and misallocation of resources on capital expenditures can divert funds away from other essential areas, such as patient care, staffing, or maintenance of existing equipment.

Second, the decisions regarding capital expenditures are strategic and have long-term implications on the hospital's ability to provide high-quality care. Investing in the latest medical technology, for example, can significantly enhance diagnostic and treatment capabilities, improve patient outcomes, and increase efficiency. However, such investments must be carefully weighed against their cost, potential return on investment, and the hospital's strategic goals.

Furthermore, capital expenditures must align with regulatory requirements and standards for patient care and safety. Hospitals must ensure that any new construction, renovation, or acquisition of medical equipment complies with these standards to maintain accreditation and avoid legal or regulatory penalties.

Lastly, these decisions often require complex considerations involving technology adoption, integration with existing systems, and training needs. A misstep in evaluating these factors can lead to underutilized investments, increased operational costs, or even adverse impacts on patient care. Thus, hospital administrators must meticulously scrutinize capital expenditures to ensure they are making informed, strategic decisions that will benefit the organization and its patients in the long run.

First you have to look at the return on investment. Central to that evaluation is reimbursement from various payors (insurance companies and federal payors such as Medicare. From there I moved to get accurate with the volumes that the investment will produce as well as the how likely is the equipment or service to stand the test of time. Technology changes at light speed and equipment can be moth balled if a there are new technologies coming down the pipe. A key question that requires research to make sure that the investment will stay relevant long enough to get the ROI you want to provide to the facility.

Focusing on Return on Investment (ROI) is crucial for hospital administrators for several intertwined financial, operational, and strategic reasons. Firstly, hospitals operate in a financially constrained environment where efficient use of resources is paramount. A strong ROI on investments, whether in new medical technologies, facility upgrades, or health information systems, ensures that the hospital utilizes its limited capital in ways that maximize financial returns. This is especially important because it enables the reinvestment of profits into areas that can further improve patient care, attract more patients, and enhance the hospital's reputation.

Secondly, demonstrating a positive ROI is vital for justifying expenditures to stakeholders, including board members, investors, and regulatory bodies. Stakeholders are more likely to support initiatives that are shown to contribute to the hospital's financial health and its ability to provide high-quality care. This support is crucial for securing funding for future projects and maintaining the hospital's operational license and accreditation.

Moreover, focusing on ROI helps hospital administrators prioritize projects that align with the hospital's strategic goals, such as improving patient outcomes, increasing efficiency, or expanding services. Investments with a high ROI can provide competitive advantages by differentiating the hospital in terms of quality of care, operational efficiency, or technological advancement.

Lastly, in the context of healthcare, ROI is not solely financial but also encompasses improvements in patient outcomes, patient satisfaction, and quality of care. By focusing on ROI, administrators can ensure that investments not only are financially prudent but also advance the hospital's mission to provide exceptional care. This holistic approach to ROI ensures that financial decisions support the broader goal of improving healthcare delivery, which is at the heart of hospital administration.

I understand that most if not all businesses have to make these evaluations, however in healthcare they come at you fast and furious. Sometimes you do have to take calculated risks to put your facility and physicians to be relied upon to provide the best services to the community you serve.

Taking calculated risks as a hospital administrator shares striking similarities with taking calculated risks in one's personal life. Both require a thorough assessment of potential outcomes, weighing the benefits against the risks, and considering the impact of decisions on both the short and long term. In a hospital setting, this might involve investing in an innovative but unproven technology that could revolutionize patient care, akin to an individual deciding to change careers based on future industry trends. Just as in life, where taking calculated risks can lead to personal growth and achievement, in hospital administration, such risks can lead to advancements in healthcare delivery, improved patient outcomes, and organizational growth, setting the stage for a legacy of innovation and leadership.

I would segue next into the power and necessity to delegate and trust your support staff. It is impractical to become an expert in radiology, cardiology, orthopaedics etc. So, developing trust with clinical experts is vital. I would always make sure that they understood what I was evaluating prior to seeking their advice.

Having good relationships with clinical experts is crucial for hospital administrators because it bridges the gap between administrative objectives and medical expertise. Given the vast and specialized knowledge required in fields such as radiology, cardiology, and orthopedics, it's impractical for an administrator to achieve expertise in all clinical areas. These relationships facilitate informed decision-making, ensuring that administrative strategies align with clinical realities and ultimately enhance patient care. By leveraging the expertise of clinicians, administrators can make better-informed decisions that support both the hospital's operational efficiency and its mission to provide high-quality healthcare.

In leadership, having confidence in one's abilities is essential to make decisive and effective decisions. However, it's equally important to recognize the limits of one's knowledge and experience. Being humble enough to ask for help not only demonstrates a commitment to making the best possible decisions for the organization but also fosters a culture of collaboration and mutual respect. This balance between confidence and humility can lead to more innovative solutions and a stronger, more cohesive team.

I also think it is key to get the advice and explore your direction with payors. Payors have different agendas including reviewing the impact that you direction has on controlling utilization and quality to their covered patients.

As a hospital executive, controlling utilization and ensuring quality care for our covered patients are paramount to both our mission and our financial viability. Proper utilization management ensures that patients receive the right level of care at the right time, avoiding unnecessary services that can drive up healthcare costs without improving outcomes. This approach not only helps in managing the hospital's resources more efficiently but also aligns with payor expectations and regulations, ensuring that the care provided is both necessary and cost-effective. By focusing on the appropriate use of medical services, we can enhance patient satisfaction and outcomes, which in turn strengthens our reputation and the trust our community places in us.

Ensuring quality care is equally critical, as it directly impacts patient health and the hospital's performance metrics. High-quality care leads to better patient outcomes, reduced readmission rates, and fewer medical errors, all of which are key factors in payor reimbursements and the hospital's financial health. It fosters a culture of excellence that attracts top medical talent and elevates the standard of care provided. Furthermore, in an era where patient satisfaction scores are publicly reported and closely linked to reimbursement rates, prioritizing quality care is not just a moral obligation but a strategic imperative that influences our hospital's success and sustainability.

Expecting payors to endorse reimbursement for services that don't result in decrease in mortality or other costly complications as well as a reduction in length of stay in hospitals specifically is not a great idea.

This shift is driven by the recognition that simply providing more services does not necessarily equate to better outcomes for patients. Payors, including insurance companies and government programs, are now focusing on endorsing reimbursements for services that demonstrate clear benefits in terms of patient outcomes, such as decreased mortality rates, fewer costly complications, and reduced lengths of hospital stays. The reasons this approach is considered prudent include:

Cost Efficiency:

Payors are under pressure to manage healthcare costs effectively. Reimbursing for services that do not contribute to significant improvements in patient outcomes can lead to increased healthcare expenses without corresponding benefits. By prioritizing payments for services that result in better health outcomes, payors can ensure more efficient use of resources.

Quality of Care:

This reimbursement strategy encourages hospitals and health-care providers to focus on the quality of care rather than the quantity of services provided. It incentivizes healthcare facilities to adopt evidence-based practices and interventions that have been proven to enhance patient outcomes.

Patient Outcomes: Ultimately, the goal of healthcare is to improve patient health. By tying reimbursement to measurable improvements in outcomes, such as reduced mortality or shorter hospital stays, payors can help drive improvements in the healthcare system that directly benefit patients.

Healthcare Sustainability: As healthcare costs continue to rise, ensuring the sustainability of healthcare systems is of paramount importance. Focusing on reimbursing services that provide real value in terms of patient outcomes helps to create a more sustainable healthcare ecosystem that can continue to meet the needs of the population.

In summary, expecting payors to endorse reimbursement for services without clear evidence of their impact on improving patient outcomes or reducing healthcare costs is not aligned with the current direction of healthcare financing. This approach helps to ensure that healthcare spending is directed towards interventions that offer tangible benefits to patients and contribute to the overall efficiency and effectiveness of the healthcare system.

I would like to see a greater initiative between payors and provider to sync up these goals. Historically the agendas of payors and providers were at odds. This is a fundamental mistake. This feels like tall order given the financial incentives of all parties, however to do anything but seeking consensus moving forward will result in increased expenses and continued fragmentation. To summarize, effective executive need to meet and communicate early and often with Payors who have significant financial risks in authorizing and providing payment care.

In a hospital setting, the collaboration between payors and providers is pivotal for enhancing patient care. This cooperative model promotes an integrated approach to healthcare, focusing on preventive measures and the efficient management of chronic conditions. Through shared data and insights, payors and providers can proactively address care gaps, leading to improved health outcomes. This synergy ensures that patients receive timely and appropriate treatments, enhancing their overall healthcare experience.

Cost efficiency is another significant benefit of a collaborative relationship between payors and providers. Together, they can identify cost-saving opportunities without compromising the quality of care, such as adopting more streamlined care models and reducing unnecessary procedures. This partnership not only helps in lowering healthcare costs but also benefits the broader ecosystem, including patients who may face lower out-of-pocket expenses and insurers and providers who can operate more efficiently.

Moreover, collaboration fosters innovation in healthcare delivery, particularly in the development of value-based care models. These models emphasize patient outcomes over the volume of services provided, encouraging providers to focus on preventive care and effective management of chronic diseases. Such innovations can lead to a reduction in the need for expensive interventions and hospitalizations, further driving down healthcare costs and improving patient care quality.

Ultimately, a collaborative approach between payors and providers increases satisfaction and trust within the healthcare system. It allows for a more aligned set of goals and facilitates the resolution of disputes in a constructive manner. This leads to higher provider satisfaction by reducing administrative burdens and making reimbursement processes more transparent. For patients, the benefits are clear: a more efficient, transparent, and patient-centered healthcare experience that fosters trust in the healthcare system.

11

Do Not Be Afraid to Be Bold

I think inherent in the general mind set is that entrepreneurs and risk takers in business have the world against them. Nothing is further from the truth. Yes, business fail. However, it is fascinating how many thrive in the face of many times bad odds. Examples are numerous. Here they are below:

Apple Inc.:

In the late 1990s, Apple was struggling with financial losses, a declining market share, and a lack of direction. It was considered nearly bankrupt and irrelevant in the computing industry. The return of Steve Jobs in 1997 marked the beginning of a dramatic turnaround, starting with the launch of the innovative iMac in 1998, followed by the iPod, iPhone, and iPad. These products revolutionized several tech sectors and propelled Apple to become one of the most valuable companies in the world.

Netflix:

In its early days, Netflix was a DVD rental service facing stiff competition from Blockbuster and other rental stores. When it first pitched the idea of streaming to Blockbuster, it was laughed out of the room. However, Netflix's pivot to streaming video over the internet in 2007, ahead of major trends in digital consumption, turned its fortunes around. Despite challenges, including a significant customer backlash over pricing changes in 2011, Netflix persevered to become a dominant force in global entertainment.

LEGO:

In the early 2000s, LEGO faced a dire financial crisis due to over-expansion and lack of focus, which diluted its brand and alienated core customers. By 2004, it was on the verge of bankruptcy. The company refocused on its core product lines and engaged more directly with its fan base, leading to a remarkable recovery. Innovations such as LEGO movies, video games, and new product lines helped turn LEGO into the world's most powerful toy company.

Starbucks:

In 2008, Starbucks appeared to be in trouble. Overexpansion and the financial crisis led to declining sales and the closure of many locations. The return of Howard Schultz as CEO in 2008 marked the beginning of a strategic turnaround that focused on improving the customer experience, expanding internationally, and innovating its product offerings. These efforts paid off, and Starbucks regained its position as a leading global coffeehouse chain.

Airbnb:

In its early days, Airbnb struggled to gain traction. The founders sold cereal boxes to fund the company when they were turned down by investors who didn't see the potential in their idea of renting out spaces in homes. However, persistence and the ability to capitalize on the sharing economy trend helped Airbnb to eventually become a major disruptor in the travel and hospitality industry.

These examples show how resilience, innovation, strategic pivoting, and sometimes a bit of luck can help businesses overcome significant obstacles and achieve remarkable success.

I submit to you that the moment an enterprise is created that momentum is provided for it to grow and many times thrive. It is unnatural for it to go backwards or remain stagnant.

In the dynamic landscape of business, a well-constructed company experiencing early growth rarely finds itself stagnant. Such firms are typically built on a foundation of innovation, adaptability, and a keen understanding of market needs, which fuels their continual expansion and evolution. The momentum gathered from early successes often propels these companies forward, as they leverage new technologies, enter unexplored markets, and refine their offerings in response to customer feedback. This state of constant motion not only characterizes their growth trajectories but also defines their corporate ethos, making stagnation an unlikely scenario.

Moreover, the leadership in these thriving companies understands the importance of reinvesting in their core competencies while exploring new avenues for growth. They are adept at navigating the challenges that come with scaling, such as maintaining company culture, ensuring operational efficiency, and meeting increasing market demands. By fostering a culture of continuous improvement and innovation, these companies set themselves apart from competitors and remain relevant in a fast-paced and ever-changing business environment. Thus, for well-built companies in the throes of early growth, stagnation is not a pitfall but a challenge to be strategically avoided through foresight, agility, and relentless pursuit of excellence.

I wanted to bring this concept forward because I hope it can provide some level of confidence in fearful circumstances. Be Brave. Be Bold. And Be Responsible.

Companies need to be bold to stand out in a crowded and competitive marketplace, where playing it safe often leads to mediocrity rather than market leadership. Boldness in strategy, innovation, and decision-making enables businesses to break new ground, redefine markets, and capture the imagination of consumers. This approach not only helps in differentiating a company from its rivals but also in fostering a culture of innovation that can propel the company to new heights. Moreover, taking calculated risks is essential for growth and adaptation, especially in industries characterized by rapid technological changes and shifting consumer preferences.

As mentioned earlier, one striking example of this is Netflix. In the late 2000s, Netflix made a daring pivot from its DVD rental service to streaming, a move that was far from guaranteed success at the time. Betting big on the future of internet entertainment, Netflix transitioned to a streaming-first business model, investing heavily in content creation and distribution infrastructure. This bold strategy not only revolutionized the entertainment industry, making Netflix a global leader in streaming media but also exemplified how a company's willingness to embrace risk and innovate can redefine an entire industry.

Case in point is Crypto. Who thought that a coin such as Bitcoin would create so much wealth since 2008? The majority of investors knew close to nothing about it. The correlations to the development of the United States stock market in 1817. Many were doubtful and felt it was some kind of Ponzi effort. The wealth and capital that it has provided has been a massive part of our history in the United States and provided a template for many other countries. If you build it they will come.

The advent of cryptocurrency has mirrored the skepticism and volatility that surrounded the early days of the stock market, particularly during its more formalized inception in 1817 with the establishment of the New York Stock Exchange (NYSE). Just as the early stock market faced widespread doubt over its viability and fears of speculation, so too has the cryptocurrency market. Skeptics of both eras questioned the underlying value of these assets, with early critics of the stock market unsure of the stability and real-world utility of trading company shares, paralleling the modern skepticism towards the tangible value and long-term sustainability of cryptocurrencies. This skepticism has been fueled by dramatic price fluctuations, speculative trading, and concerns over regulatory oversight in both markets.

Additionally, the transformative potential of both markets was initially underestimated. In the early 19th century, the stock market began to lay the groundwork for modern corporate finance, enabling companies to raise capital more efficiently and providing investors with a stake in future profits. Similarly, cryptocurrency has introduced a radical shift in traditional finance, offering decentralized finance (DeFi) solutions, smart contracts, and the potential for greater financial inclusion. Both innovations initially faced dismissal as fads or overly speculative ventures, only for their enduring impact on the financial landscape to become more apparent over time.

Moreover, both the early stock market and the cryptocurrency market have experienced cycles of booms and busts that tested investor confidence and regulatory resolve. The Panic of 1819, for example, was partly attributed to speculative investments in the stock market, much like how various cryptocurrency crashes have been linked to speculative excesses. Despite these challenges, both markets have demonstrated resilience and adaptability, gradually earning a degree of acceptance and integration into the broader financial ecosystem. Just as the stock market matured and became central to global economics, cryptocurrency is increasingly seen as a legitimate, though still evolving, component of the financial world, highlighting the cyclical nature of financial innovation and market adaptation.

These tendencies are accelerated when the business provides needed goods or services. I think that so many more people or businesses want you to win. That energy gets transmitted. When a business successfully balances the act of serving its customers while also securing its financial objectives, a positive energy permeates the organization, fostering a culture of success and satisfaction. This synergy arises because employees feel motivated and engaged, knowing their efforts contribute to both customer happiness and the company's prosperity. Customers, in turn, sense the company's commitment to quality and value, which builds loyalty and trust, reinforcing a virtuous cycle of repeat business and positive word-of-mouth. Ultimately, this dynamic creates a sustainable model where the company's financial health and customer satisfaction feed into each other, driving continuous growth and innovation.

12

To Consent Is Not to Be Weak

The concept of Consensus is so often overlooked. I feel like the lessening of authoritative management has been re-designed over the last 20 years. The chain of command model will likely never go away however the doctrine has shifted and movement towards giving employees more autonomy and being given a voice without fear of mutiny has grown and is a good thing. Of course, the "Buck has to Stop" somewhere. But it's how the Buck stops that matters. In a diverse on all levels as a hospital is. You need to hear all perspectives even if you don't think all perspectives are necessary. The best way to disable someone is to invalidate their opinion. That doesn't sound like a good idea for anyone that you rely on to move your goals forward.

In the world of business, the art of listening and the process of building consensus are foundational for achieving long-term success and fostering a collaborative environment. "Most people do not listen with the intent to understand; they listen with the intent to reply," remarked Stephen R. Covey, highlighting a common barrier in effective communication. When leaders and team members prioritize understanding each other's perspectives, they pave the way for innovative

93

solutions that might not emerge from a single viewpoint. This process not only enriches the decision-making process but also ensures that strategies are more robust and inclusive, reflecting the collective wisdom and insight of the entire team.

Moreover, building consensus is critical in navigating the complexities of today's business challenges. It ensures that decisions are made considering diverse viewpoints, leading to more sustainable and effective outcomes. "If you make listening and observation your occupation, you will gain much more than you can by talk," the wise words of Robert Baden-Powell remind us. Through active listening and seeking common ground, businesses can foster a culture of respect and mutual understanding, which is essential for driving engagement, innovation, and adaptability in a rapidly changing market landscape.

Ultimately, the practice of listening deeply to others and forging consensus is not just about achieving immediate business goals; it's about building a resilient and adaptive organizational culture. "The most basic of all human needs is the need to understand and be understood. The best way to understand people is to listen to them," noted Ralph G. Nichols. This timeless advice underscores the significance of listening as the cornerstone of effective communication and leadership. By embedding these principles into their core operations, businesses can navigate challenges more effectively, foster a strong sense of community and purpose among their teams, and achieve sustainable growth in an ever-evolving business environment.

Some of this concept involves simple manners. For instance, it is a bad idea to go into a group that you know has different ideas and slam one side or the other. By default, you will make half the group angry at a minimum. You can't get much done from there. I understand this requires a level of diplomacy because the ball you are moving, they may not fully understand. Perfecting the team process in management of any kind should be gratifying for each member. Tell them why they are important because of their knowledge, skills and experience.

Again, your company is like an army. Building up each and every part of the army is crucial for overall military effectiveness, a lesson underscored by several American wars throughout history. These examples illustrate the importance of a well-rounded and fully supported military force in achieving strategic objectives.

The American Civil War (1861-1865):

This conflict highlighted the critical role of logistics and infrastructure alongside combat operations. The Union's ability to effectively organize, equip, and mobilize its naval and ground forces, along with superior railroad and telegraphic communications, contributed significantly to its ultimate victory. The Confederacy, despite having skilled generals and motivated troops, struggled with the logistics of supplying and reinforcing their armies, which ultimately contributed to their defeat. This underscored the necessity of a comprehensive approach to military buildup, where logistics and support systems are as prioritized as frontline troops.

World War II (1939-1945):

The United States' involvement in World War II demonstrated the importance of industrial and technological superiority in addition to sheer military might. The ability to produce vast quantities of war material and innovate technologically (e.g., the development of radar and the atomic bomb) played a decisive role in the Allied victory. This period showed that every sector of the military, from infantry and armor to air forces and naval power, needed to be well-supported and equipped with the latest technology to ensure success across different theaters of war.

The Vietnam War (1955-1975):

The Vietnam War emphasized the importance of guerrilla warfare tactics and the need for specialized units trained in counter-insurgency operations. Despite having superior technology and firepower, the U.S. military found itself challenged by the Viet Cong's guerrilla tactics. This conflict highlighted the necessity of having diverse capabilities within the military, including intelligence, psychological operations, and local population engagement strategies, in addition to conventional forces.

These examples from American military history demonstrate that success in warfare requires more than just having a large number of troops; it demands a holistic approach to military buildup. This includes ensuring that all branches and units are well-equipped, well-trained, and supported with adequate logistics, intelligence, and technology. The complexity of modern warfare further amplifies the need for a comprehensive and balanced military force capable of meeting a wide range of challenges.

I recall an instance on a major capital expense Medivax helicopter. The hospital was about 3 hours from major cities with provisions for much more complex patient care primarily Trauma. I thought it was cool as hell, however it was pricey. While I worked on projections to justify the purchase I was hitting a brick wall. Our company was extremely well run financially and didn't take unnecessary risk. At the end of the day, we couldn't justify it. I watched out CEO evaluate the entire management team's response and input as he stayed for the most part neutral. There was the typical division among clinical staff and financial people. There was quite a gulf. In the end, we couldn't justify it based on projected volume. The return on investment was decades long. Beyond the debt, the service and maintenance was very expensive. This is why tax supported hospitals typically provide this many times lifesaving service. We couldn't get consensus on the spend.

Companies, including hospitals, should exercise caution when contemplating bold moves that come with a high risk of financial loss due to several critical factors. For hospitals, the stakes are even higher because their decisions can directly affect patient care, access to essential health services, and community well-being.

Firstly, hospitals operate in an inherently sensitive and critical sector where the primary mission is to provide healthcare services rather than maximize profit. Any financial instability resulting from risky ventures could compromise their ability to deliver high-quality care, access to the latest medical technologies, and the maintenance of essential staff. Financial health in the healthcare sector is directly tied to operational capacity and service quality, making excessive financial risks particularly perilous.

Secondly, the healthcare industry is subject to extensive regulation and oversight, making any significant changes or bold moves a complex process that involves navigating legal, ethical, and compliance landscapes. Financial losses from ventures that don't pan out can not only strain resources but also potentially lead to regulatory scrutiny if they affect the hospital's ability to meet its obligations and standards of care.

Furthermore, hospitals and healthcare institutions often rely on the trust and confidence of the communities they serve. Taking on high-risk financial ventures can jeopardize that trust, especially if the pursuit of profit is seen to come at the expense of patient care or if it leads to cuts in essential services. Public perception is crucial in healthcare, as it can influence patient choices, philanthropic donations, and community support.

Lastly, the financial frameworks within which hospitals operate are complex, with funding coming from a variety of sources including government programs, insurance reimbursements, and private payments. Bold moves that risk significant financial loss can disrupt these delicate financial balances and lead to increased costs for patients, reduced services, or even the closure of hospital units or entire facilities, particularly in areas where healthcare options are already limited.

In summary, while innovation and adaptability are important for hospitals to meet changing healthcare needs, they must approach bold financial moves with caution. The imperative to do no harm extends beyond patient care to the financial decisions that underpin the availability and quality of healthcare services.

I promise to not get political in this book however, it is hard to ignore that our leaders have set extremely bad examples on the topic of consensus. You must look back decades to even find many that tried. I urge executives to use the power of consensus to reach or achieve goals. It is a secret weapon in management and too often ignored.

In U.S. politics, the inability of Republicans and Democrats to reach consensus has often led to significant gridlocks, impacting governance and policy implementation. Here are a few notable examples:

Government Shutdowns:

Perhaps the most visible consequence of partisan deadlock is the government shutdown. For instance, the 2013 shutdown lasted for 16 days, stemming from a dispute over the Affordable Care Act (often referred to as Obamacare). Republicans, controlling the House of Representatives, sought to defund or delay the act as part of the federal budget process. Democrats, with a majority in the Senate and the presidency under Barack Obama, refused these conditions, leading to a stalemate that temporarily closed federal agencies and furloughed thousands of employees.

Debt Ceiling Crises:

The debt ceiling debates have repeatedly showcased deep divides between the parties, particularly in 2011 and again in 2013, where Republicans pushed for significant spending cuts in exchange for agreeing to raise the national debt limit, while Democrats advocated for increasing revenues to address deficits. The 2011 crisis led to the first-ever downgrade of the U.S. credit rating by Standard & Poor's, citing the political brinkmanship and the government's difficulty in addressing medium-term fiscal challenges.

Supreme Court Nominations:

The nomination process for Supreme Court justices has become increasingly contentious, reflecting deep partisan divides. A notable instance is the refusal by Senate Republicans in 2016 to consider President Obama's nominee, Merrick Garland, to the Supreme Court, arguing that the next president should make the appointment since it was an election year. This move was seen as a stark example of how partisan gridlock can halt the normal functioning of government responsibilities.

Immigration Reform:

Efforts to reform the U.S. immigration system have frequently been thwarted by partisan divisions. In 2013, a comprehensive immigration reform bill passed the Senate with bipartisan support but was not brought to a vote in the Republican-controlled House, due in part to disagreements over provisions related to border security and pathways to citizenship for undocumented immigrants. The inability to reconcile these differences has left many aspects of U.S. immigration policy in a state of uncertainty and stasis.

These examples underscore how political polarization and the inability to build consensus between Republicans and Democrats can lead to significant disruptions in government operations and policy implementation, affecting a wide range of issues from fiscal policy to social justice and governance norms.

Like the United States government, hospitals operate in a complex, high-stakes environment where finding consensus on sensitive issues is crucial for maintaining optimal operation. In the realm of healthcare, where decisions can have immediate and profound impacts on patient well-being, achieving consensus among medical professionals, administrators, and stakeholders ensures that policies and practices are both medically sound and aligned with the institution's values and goals. This collaborative approach facilitates a unified front in tackling challenges such as resource allocation, ethical dilemmas, and the integration of innovative treatments, thereby preventing gridlock that can compromise patient care. Just as political consensus is key to effective governance, in hospitals, it underpins the delivery of high-quality, consistent, and equitable healthcare services. By striving for consensus on sensitive issues, hospitals can navigate the complexities of healthcare delivery more effectively, ensuring that they continue to operate at an impressive level, even in the face of emerging challenges and diverse viewpoints.

13

The Secret Weapon: Delegation

Much a been written about delegation. My primary observation: start with the fundamentals. Management is full of people that struggle with the concept. First, it requires a comfort to give up control to a certain degree which many struggle with that out of the shoot. The trait or characteristic of not having strong delegation skills will determine the size and success of your organization. Without proper delegation, the following can occur:

Overburdened Leadership:

Without proper delegation, leaders and managers can become overwhelmed with tasks that could be effectively handled by their team members. This can lead to burnout, reduced effectiveness in decision-making, and a bottleneck effect, where progress on projects stalls because everything requires the leader's input or approval.

Underutilized Talent:

Employees who are not given responsibilities commensurate with their skills and abilities are underutilized. This can lead to dissatisfaction and demotivation, as team members feel their potential is not being recognized or harnessed. Over time, this can result in decreased employee engagement and productivity.

Inhibited Team Development:

Delegation is a key tool in developing team members by providing them with opportunities to take on new challenges, learn new skills, and grow in their roles. Without it, employees may find their growth opportunities limited, leading to stagnation in their professional development and potentially causing the organization to fall behind its competitors.

Poor Morale and Company Culture:

A lack of delegation can contribute to a culture where employees feel micromanaged and undervalued. This can erode trust in leadership, reduce job satisfaction, and negatively affect morale. A toxic work culture can lead to high turnover rates, making it difficult to retain top talent.

Decreased Innovation:

When decision-making is centralized and employees are not empowered to take initiative, innovation can suffer. Diverse ideas and solutions often come from those working closely with the products, services, or customers. Without the ability to contribute or make decisions, employees are less likely to propose innovative solutions.

Inefficient Use of Resources:

Proper delegation allows for the efficient use of the organization's human resources by ensuring tasks are performed by the most appropriate person. Without it, tasks may be handled inefficiently, wasting time and resources that could be better allocated elsewhere.

Difficulty Scaling: For businesses looking to grow, the ability to delegate effectively becomes increasingly important. A failure to delegate can hamper scalability, as the organization's operations become too complex for a small group of individuals to manage directly. This can lead to missed opportunities and challenges in responding to market demands or expanding operations.

Increased Risk of Errors: Overburdened leaders and demotivated employees are more likely to make mistakes. When tasks are not delegated to individuals with the appropriate expertise, the risk of errors can increase, potentially leading to quality issues, customer dissatisfaction, and reputational damage.

To avoid these pitfalls, businesses should foster a culture of trust and empowerment, where delegation is viewed as a tool for organizational efficiency, employee development, and innovation. Developing delegation skills among managers and leaders is essential for the health and growth of any organization.

The way successful executives line up on the topic is simple. I think everyone at some point in time wishes the "there were 3 of me." The power of delegation allows that. And in many cases "500 of you" if you manage it correctly.

From an exponential viewpoint, the importance of delegation in a company can be understood through the lens of leveraging individual talent to catapult widespread organizational growth and innovation. When you have one exceptionally talented employee, their knowledge, skills, and work ethic can significantly contribute to the company's success. However, the impact of this individual is inherently limited by their capacity to work—there are only so many hours in the day, and one person can only do so much, no matter how talented.

Now, imagine if this individual's methodologies, mindset, and skills could be transferred to others within the organization. Through effective delegation, not only are tasks distributed, but so too are these valuable traits. This is where the exponential potential comes into play. Here's why:

Multiplication of Effort:

Delegating tasks allows the talented individual to focus on higher-level strategy and innovation, while others take on responsibilities that utilize and enhance their skills. This is not just additive in terms of productivity; it's multiplicative, as each delegated task frees up strategic bandwidth for innovation and growth.

Knowledge Transfer and Upskilling:

By delegating responsibilities, the talented individual can mentor others, transferring their skills and knowledge throughout the organization. This creates a learning environment where skills are continuously developed, and the overall capability of the organization grows exponentially over time.

Innovation and Problem Solving:

With more employees empowered to take on significant roles, the number of people working on solving problems and innovating increases. This doesn't just add to the pool of ideas—it exponentially increases the variety and depth of solutions and innovations the company can produce, as diverse perspectives lead to novel solutions.

Scalability:

A company that effectively delegates can scale more efficiently because it isn't as limited by the bandwidth of a few individuals. As the organization grows, the foundational systems of delegation ensure that new challenges can be met with agility and that responsibilities can be quickly distributed to the most capable individuals.

Resilience through Redundancy:

By spreading knowledge and skills across multiple employees, the company is less vulnerable to the loss of any single individual. This redundancy means that the organization is more resilient and can continue to operate effectively even as personnel changes occur.

Engagement and Morale:

Delegation also empowers employees, leading to higher engagement and morale. Empowered employees are more likely to feel valued and invested in the company's success, further driving productivity and innovation.

Exponential Growth:

As more individuals within the company learn and adopt the high-performance habits of the talented employee, the growth of the company can shift from linear to exponential. Each new project or initiative undertaken by these empowered employees has the potential to significantly impact the company's success.

In essence, the exponential importance of delegation in a company lies in its ability to amplify talent, knowledge, and innovation across the organization, turning individual potential into collective success. Through this multiplier effect, companies can achieve levels of growth and innovation that far surpass what would be possible through the efforts of any one individual, no matter how talented.

Delegation requires skills, communication along with a structure of accountability that allows for your success and the folks that get the opportunity to implement on your behalf. I think the threshold question in the hiring process needs to be am I comfortable hiring this person based on their ability to be able to handle delegated task and assist you to grow the organization.

If you're the CEO of a company and you're considering hiring someone to whom you would not be willing to delegate tasks, it's important to reassess the decision to hire that person in the first place. This scenario highlights several key considerations about the role of delegation in leadership and the implications of not utilizing it effectively:

Waste of Resources:

Hiring someone without delegating tasks to them represents a significant waste of resources. Salaries, training, and the time invested in recruitment are substantial costs to the company. If the employee is not effectively utilized, these resources are not generating the return they should, impacting the company's profitability and efficiency.

Underutilization of Talent:

Employees are hired for their skills, experience, and potential contribution to the company. Not delegating tasks to them means their talents are underutilized. This not only demotivates the employee but also deprives the company of the value the employee could bring to the organization.

Bottlenecking Decision-making and Productivity:

As a CEO, your time and attention are limited and should be focused on strategic decision-making and leadership. Not delegating operational tasks and decisions creates a bottleneck, slowing down productivity and responsiveness. This can hamper the company's ability to adapt to changes and seize opportunities in a timely manner.

Stifling Employee Growth and Engagement:

Delegation is not just about distributing work; it's also a tool for employee development. By entrusting employees with responsibilities, you help them grow their skills, confidence, and capacity to contribute more significantly to the company. Without delegation, employees miss out on these growth opportunities, leading to lower engagement and job satisfaction.

Impairing Team and Organizational Culture:

A reluctance to delegate can signal a lack of trust in your team's abilities, which can undermine morale and create a culture of dependency where employees feel unable to make decisions or take initiative. This diminishes the sense of empowerment and accountability that drives high-performing teams.

Limiting Organizational Scalability:

A company that doesn't delegate effectively will struggle to scale. The ability to delegate tasks efficiently is crucial for managing an increasing workload as the company grows. Without this, every new challenge or opportunity requires direct CEO involvement, which is not sustainable.

Risk of Burnout:

Concentrating too many responsibilities on the CEO's shoulders is not just inefficient; it's also risky. The stress and workload can lead to burnout, affecting decision-making, leadership quality, and ultimately, the well-being of the CEO.

Therefore, as a CEO, if you find yourself unwilling to delegate tasks to a potential hire, it's crucial to examine the reasons behind this reluctance. Is it a lack of trust in the individual's abilities, a desire to maintain control, or perhaps a misunderstanding of the role's requirements? Addressing these concerns is essential not only for the health of the organization but also for ensuring that the company can grow and thrive in a competitive landscape.

As for the design and management of the delegation process which is Chief among the responsibilities of leadership, I recommend the following: keeping the categories as simple as possible i.e., rank them in order of importance to the organization, maybe one through three. Place your most competent and experienced people on and schedule more than less experienced and more talented employees. We have seen examples recently where staff makes decisions based on personal beliefs rather than those that are in the best interest of the company and they have been so off base it costs the company a lot. That is an example of delegating poorly. Then you have an embarrassing mess to fix.

Making decisions in a business based solely on gut feeling, rather than on the actual circumstances and data within the company, can be perilous. As the philosopher Socrates once said, "An unexamined life is not worth living." This wisdom extends to business decision-making, where an unexamined strategy can lead to failure. Relying solely on intuition ignores the rich insights that can be gained from analyzing company data, market trends, and customer feedback. It can lead to misaligned priorities and overlooked opportunities, as intuition might not always align with the reality of the market or the internal state of the company. Without evidence to back decisions, the business risks making moves that are not just unwise, but potentially destructive.

Furthermore, decision-making based solely on gut feeling undermines the collective intelligence and expertise of the company's team. Friedrich Nietzsche once remarked, "*All things are subject to interpretation whichever interpretation prevails at a given time is a function of power and not truth.*" When a leader relies only on their gut, they may be imposing their subjective interpretation of situations without considering the broader perspectives and insights their team could offer. This approach can stifle innovation and employee engagement, as team members feel their knowledge and insights are undervalued. Ultimately, decisions made without a grounding in the reality of the company's operations and environment are more about exerting power than finding the best path forward, limiting the company's ability to adapt and thrive in a competitive landscape.

The Covid pandemic threw thousands of curve balls at our society. My circumstance was somewhat unique. I am on the executive staff of a great High-Complexity Diagnostic lab in New Orleans. If you remember, there was a massive the spike in cases following Mardi Gras in 2020. The variant at that time was nasty and took a lot of souls away from us. We had the capability to do the gold standard PCR tests and we did a lot of them, many for the TV/Film industry which Louisiana does a lot primarily because of tax incentives but also its diverse geography.

Opportunities that present themselves rarely in life are akin to rare gems; their value lies not just in their scarcity but in the transformative potential they hold. Just as Seneca the Younger, a Roman Stoic philosopher, famously said, "Luck is what happens when preparation meets opportunity," the essence of seizing rare opportunities is about being prepared to leap when they arise. In life, these moments can define our trajectory, offering paths to personal growth, fulfilment, or the realization of our dreams. Ignoring such opportunities out of fear or hesitation can lead to a lifetime of wondering "what if?" Similarly, in the business world, these rare opportunities—whether they're breakthrough innovations, market gaps, or strategic partnerships—require swift and decisive action. Failing to capitalize on them can mean missing out on a pivotal moment that could elevate a company from a contender to a leader in its field.

In both life and business, the principle of seizing rare opportunities is underpinned by the understanding that time and chance are fleeting. As the philosopher H. Jackson Brown Jr. noted, "Opportunity dances with those already on the dance floor." This metaphor beautifully encapsulates the idea that being active, engaged, and ready is crucial for taking advantage of rare *opportunities* when they present themselves. In life, this could mean embracing change or making bold decisions that lead to new adventures and personal growth. In business, it translates to staying vigilant, innovative, and agile qualities that enable a company to pivot or scale when unique opportunities arise. Just as in life, a business that hesitates or fails to recognize and act on these rare chances may miss out on transformative growth or industry leadership, underscoring the universal truth that opportunity favors the prepared and the bold.

We had a good reputation and were comfortable not only getting the testing done but resulting them to keep up with their pace and compliance standards. As word traveled, I started to get request for various productions in Texas and was a bit overwhelmed. I have a terrible inability to say no. With demand so high, I knew I needed to get some good people that could help me when I couldn't be at many places at once.

Hiring the right people is crucial, especially when a business is poised to capitalize on a significant opportunity. The individuals within the organization are the primary drivers of its success; they execute strategies, interact with customers, and create the products or services the business offers. When a company faces a pivotal opportunity—such as entering a new market, launching a new product, or scaling operations—the need for a team that is not only skilled but also aligned with the company's culture and goals becomes even more critical. The right employees can accelerate growth, bring innovative ideas to fruition, and effectively manage the increased workload that often comes with seizing such opportunities. Conversely, the wrong hires can hinder progress, dilute the company's culture, and even cause strategic initiatives to fail, thereby squandering the opportunity at hand.

Moreover, in the realm of business, the impact of hiring the right people during times of opportunity cannot be overstated. As Jim

Collins famously said in his book *Good to Great*, "Get the right people on the bus, and the wrong people off the bus, and then figure out where to drive it." This principle highlights the importance of assembling a team with the right mix of talent and temperament before pushing forward with significant growth initiatives. Right hires bring with them the resilience, adaptability, and commitment needed to navigate the challenges of scaling operations or transforming the business. They are catalysts for innovation and efficiency, vital for maintaining momentum and achieving competitive advantage when opportunities arise. Thus, investing time and resources in attracting, hiring, and retaining the right people is essential for any business aiming to make the most of a significant opportunity.

I was fortunate for sure, but I found great people to help and delegate to handle the jobs that came up so I could press on the marketing side. I think we all knew that the demand had a life span as the virus mutated. I was most interested in people that could represent well with confidence and competence. So many of our client base were frankly scared. And I wanted people associated with my company to provide a calming presence at the same time giving them the best state of the art testing results available. Had I not delegated tasks my revenue it would have been four times less if not more. Delegation creates revenue and time something that puts pace and growth in your control.

Conclusion

As we draw the curtains on this journey through the corridors of healthcare leadership and personal evolution, I find myself reflecting on the immense responsibilities and unforeseen challenges that accompany the role of a healthcare executive. This memoir has not just been a recounting of trials and triumphs but a blueprint for those who aspire to lead, innovate, and impact lives in healthcare and beyond. Like a ship navigating through tempestuous waters, a leader in healthcare must maintain composure and vision, steering towards the beacon of improved patient care and organizational excellence.

"Man is only truly great when he acts from his passions," said Benjamin Disraeli. It was passion that drove us during the tumultuous times of reform, akin to the civil rights movement—a pivotal moment in U.S. history where perseverance and dedication led to profound societal change. Similarly, healthcare leaders must anchor their actions in the passion for betterment, equity, and compassion, championing reforms even when faced with formidable opposition.

I've said it earlier, but I'll mention it again right now. The wisdom of Socrates, who advocated for the pursuit of knowledge through questioning, resonates deeply with the essence of healthcare leadership. "The unexamined life is not worth living," he declared, and so it is with our practices and policies within hospital management. Continuous improvement and introspection are vital, just as they were during the transformative years following the signing of the Declaration of Independence. Those leaders embraced uncertainty with courage and a vision for a better future—qualities essential for any executive facing the shifting paradigms of healthcare.

To the future healthcare executives, business owners, and entrepreneurs who might glean wisdom from these pages, remember that leadership is not just about steering the ship but about understanding the sea. As John F. Kennedy profoundly stated during the space race, a time when innovation and bold leadership propelled humanity to new frontiers, "We choose to go to the moon in this decade and do the other things, not because they are easy, but because they are hard." The path of leadership is fraught with challenges, but it is our willingness to tackle these challenges head-on that defines our legacy.

Innovation in healthcare, much like in any business, must be approached with both a bold spirit and a meticulous eye for detail. Reflect on the lessons from the Industrial Revolution, an era of great innovation and also of significant disruption. As leaders, we must drive innovation that is not only groundbreaking but also sustainable and sensitive to the human dimensions of healthcare.

Furthermore, let us not forget the importance of empathy and ethical leadership, principles that are as unyielding as the laws that govern our land. "Ethics is knowing the difference between what you have a right to do and what is right to do," Potter Stewart once said. In the realm of healthcare, where decisions can mean life or death, the moral compass of a leader must be steadfast and clear.

In closing, I urge all aspiring leaders to cultivate resilience, embrace innovation, and above all, lead with integrity. Remember, true leadership is a lifelong journey of learning and growth. It is my hope that my experiences and reflections ignite in you a flame of passion and perseverance to pursue not only the success of your institutions but the greater good of all those they serve.

May your path be guided by the profound lessons of history, the wisdom of philosophers, and an unwavering commitment to making a difference. Lead not just with the mind but with the heart, and let every step you take in leadership be a step towards a brighter, healthier future for all.

REFERENCES
Chapter 1

1.   "Ulysses". Alfred, Lord Tennyson. *Poetry Foundation.* https://www.poetryfoundation.org/poems/45392/ulysses. Retrieved March 3rd, 2024.

2.   Nicholas Crafts, Peter Fearon, Lessons from the 1930s Great Depression, Oxford Review of Economic Policy, Volume 26, Issue 3, Autumn 2010, Pages 285–317, https://doi.org/10.1093/ox-rep/grq030. Retrieved March 3rd, 2024.

3.   "Great Depression Facts. *Franklin D. Roosevelt Presidential Library and Museum.* 2016. https://www.fdrlibrary.org/great-depression-facts. Retrieved March 3rd, 2024.

4.   e Spinoza, Baruch. *The Philosophy of Spinoza*, edited by J. Ratner. USA: Tudor Publishing, [1926] 2010. p. 175

5.   HEUSTON S. The Most Famous Thing Robert E. Lee Never Said: Duty, Forgery, and Cultural Amnesia. *Journal of American Studies.* 2014;48(4):E96. doi:10.1017/S0021875814001315

6.   Bergland, Christopher. "The Importance of Self-Reliance." *Psychology Today.* January 16th, 2012. https://www.psychologytoday.com/us/blog/the-athletes-way/201201/the-importance-self-reliance. Retrieved March 3rd, 2024.

7.   "Fathers' Sons and Brothers' Keepers." Blow, Charles. February 28th, 2014. *The New York Times.*

https://www.nytimes.com/2014/03/01/opinion/blow-fathers-sons-and-brothers-keepers.html. Retrieved March 3rd, 2024.

8.   "Oxford Essential Quotations." Ratliffe, Susan. *Oxford University Press.* 2016. https://www.oxfordreference.com/display/10.1093/acref/9780191826719.001.0001/acref-9780191826719. Retrieved March 3rd, 2024.

9.   Chowdry, Amit. "Lessons Learned from 4 Steve Jobs Quotes." *Forbes.* October 5th, 2013. https://www.forbes.com/sites/amitchowdhry/2013/10/05/lessons-learned-from-4-steve-jobs-quotes/?sh=34119f124f69. Retrieved March 3rd, 2024.

10.   "Take The First Step in Faith. You Don't Have to See The Whole Staircase, Just Take The First Step." *Quote Investigator.* April 18th, 2019. https://quoteinvestigator.com/2019/04/18/staircase/. Retrieved March 3rd, 2024.

11.   "Eustress vs. distress: What is the difference?" *Medical News Today.* https://www.medicalnewstoday.com/articles/eustress-vs-distress#definitions. Retrieved March 3rd, 2024.

12.   "Conscientiousness." *Psychology Today.* https://www.psychologytoday.com/us/basics/conscientiousness. Retrieved March 3rd, 2024.

13.   "Agreeableness." *Psychology Today.* https://www.psychologytoday.com/us/basics/agreeableness. Retrieved March 3rd, 2024.

14.   US Inflation Calculator. https://www.usinflationcalculator.com/. Retrieved March 3rd, 2024.

15.   Sternberg, R. J. (1985). *Beyond IQ: A Triarchic Theory of Intelligence*. Cambridge University Press.

16.   Sternberg, R. J. (1997). "A Triarchic View of Giftedness: Theory and Practice". In Coleangelo; Davis (eds.). *Handbook of Gifted Education*. pp. 43–53.

17.   Zipkin, Nina. "10 Inspiring Quotes From Howard Schultz on Great Leadership and Business Success." *Entrepreneur.* June 5th, 2018. https://www.entrepreneur.com/business-news/10-inspiring-quotes-from-howard-schultz-on-great-leadership/314514. Retrieved March 3rd, 2024.

18.   "Oxford Essential Quotations." Ratliffe, Susan. *Oxford University Press.* 2016. https://www.oxfordreference.com/display/10.1093/acref/9780191826719.001.0001/q-oro-ed4-00008097. Retrieved March 3rd, 2024.

19.   "Divergent vs. Convergent Thinking." *Creately.* October 12th, 2023. https://creately.com/guides/divergent-vs-convergent-thinking/. Retrieved March 3rd, 2024.

20.   Dahunsi, Landre. "Book Summary – Call Me Ted" by Ted Turner. February 5th, 2021. https://lanredahunsi.com/call-me-ted-by-ted-turner/. Retrieved March 3rd, 2024.

Chapter 2

1.   Bosker, Bianca. "Sheryl Sandberg: 'There's No Such Thing As Work-Life Balance.'" *Huffington Post.* April 12th, 2012.

https://www.huffpost.com/entry/sheryl-sandberg_n_1409061. Retrieved March 4th, 2024.

2.   DerSarkissian, Carol. "Balancing Work and Family." *WebMD*. February 20th, 2024. https://www.webmd.com/balance/balancing-work-and-family. Retrieved March 4th, 2024.

3.   Crawford, N. "Employees' longer working hours linked to family conflict, stress-related health problems." *American Psychological Association*. June 2002. Vol 33. No. 6. Page 18. https://www.apa.org/monitor/jun02/employees. Retrieved March 4th, 2024.

4.   "5 Side Effects of Working Too Much." *Cleveland Clinic*. October 26th, 2024. https://health.clevelandclinic.org/effects-of-working-too-much. Retrieved March 4th, 2024.

5.   Bhandari, Smitha. "What to Know About Work and Mental Health." *WebMD*. February 25th, 2024. https://www.webmd.com/mental-health/what-to-know-about-work-and-mental-health. Retrieved March 4th, 2024.

6.   Hadden, Joey. "9 inspiring Michael Jordan quotes that will get you fired up for any challenge." *Business Insider*. May 11th, 2020. https://www.businessinsider.com/inspiring-motivational-quotes-by-michael-jordan-2020-4. Retrieved March 4th, 2024.

7.   Klein, Gary. "Cognitive Diversity: What It Is and Why It Matters." *Psychology Today*. August 16th, 2023.

https://www.psychologytoday.com/us/blog/seeing-what-others-dont/202307/cognitive-diversity-what-it-is-and-why-it-matters. Retrieved March 4th, 2024.

8.	Stillman, Jessica. "7 Jeff Bezos Quotes That Outline the Secret to Success." *Inc.* May 7th, 2014. https://www.inc.com/jessica-stillman/7-jeff-bezos-quotes-that-will-make-you-rethink-success.html. Retrieved March 4th, 2024.

Chapter 3

1.	Willer, David; Walker, Henry A. (2007). *Building Experiments: Testing Social Theory.* Stanford University Press. p. 41. ISBN 978-0-8047-5246-6.

2.	Asch, Solomon (1951). "Effects of group pressure on the modification and distortion of judgments". *Groups, Leadership and Men: Research in Human Relations.* Carnegie Press. pp. 177–190.

3.	"Facebook Founder Mark Zuckerberg Commencement Address – Harvard Commencement 2017. *YouTube.* Harvard University. https://www.youtube.com/watch?v=BmYv8XG1-YU. Retrieved March 6th, 2024.

4.	Glickman, Jodi. "When You're Younger Than the People You Manage." *Harvard Business Review.* December 24th, 2020. https://hbr.org/2020/12/when-youre-younger-than-the-people-you-manage. Retrieved March 6th, 2024.

5.   Finnegan, Pat. "Managing Older Employees As A Younger Manager: Realities to Consider." *PM Problems*. October 23, 2019. https://solvepmproblems.com/managing-older-employees-as-a-younger-manager-realities-to-consider/. Retrieved March 6th, 2024.

6.   "division of labor." *Britannica Money*. January 12th, 2024. https://www.britannica.com/money/division-of-labour. Retrieved March 6th, 2024.

Chapter 4

1.   "Battle of Yorktown." *History*. June 21st, 2023. https://www.history.com/topics/american-revolution/siege-of-yorktown. Retrieved March 6th, 2024.

2.   "Battle of Gettysburg." *History*. March 17th, 2023. https://www.history.com/topics/american-civil-war/battle-of-gettysburg. Retrieved March 6th, 2024.

3.   "Battle of Bull Run." *History*. December 11th, 2019. https://www.history.com/topics/american-civil-war/first-battle-of-bull-run. Retrieved March 6th, 2024.

4.   "Pearl Harbor." *History. December 6th, 2022.* https://www.history.com/topics/world-war-ii/pearl-harbor. Retrieved March 6th, 2024.

5.   "Why Quality of Hire is HR's Most Important Metric." *Harver*. July 20th, 2023. https://harver.com/blog/why-quality-of-hire-is-hrs-most-important-metric/. Retrieved March 6th, 2024.

6. Riggio, Ronald. "5 Reasons Why Micromanagers Fail." *Psychology Today*. August 9th, 2018. Retrieved March 6th, 2024.

7. Forbes Coaches Council. "Micromanaging? Here's How (And Why) You Should Stop." *Forbes.* https://www.forbes.com/sites/forbescoachescouncil/2017/05/19/micromanaging-heres-how-and-why-you-should-stop/?sh=e49a4777518b. Retrieved March 6th, 2024.

8. Schwantes, Marcel. "Steve Jobs Once Gave Some Brilliant Management Advice on Hiring Top People. Here It Is in 2 Sentences." *Inc.* October 17th, 2017. https://www.inc.com/marcel-schwantes/this-classic-quote-from-steve-jobs-about-hiring-employees-describes-what-great-leadership-looks-like.html. Retrieved March 6th, 2024.

9. "Alexander Hamilton and his Patron, George Washington." *PBS.* https://www.pbs.org/wgbh/americanexperience/features/hamilton-and-his-patron-george-washington. Retrieved March 6th, 2024.

10. Ott, Tim. "How George Washington Kept Alexander Hamilton in Check." *Biography.* February 14th, 2020. https://www.biography.com/political-figures/george-washington-alexander-hamilton-relationship. Retrieved March 6th, 2024.

11. *Maxims of George Washington.* Mount Vernon Ladies Association, Library. 1993.

12. "From George Washington to Lewis Nicola, 22 May 1782." https://founders.archives.gov/documents/Washington/99-01-02-08501. Retrieved March 6th, 2024.

13. Klein, Christopher. "How Lincoln and Grant's Partnership Won the Civil War." *History*. February 12th, 2024. https://www.history.com/news/abraham-lincoln-ulysses-s-grant-partnership-civil-war. Retrieved March 6th, 2024.

14. "Lincoln, Grant and Sherman Huddle Up, 150 Years ago." *History*. September 4th, 2018. https://www.history.com/news/lincoln-grant-and-sherman-huddle-up-150-years-ago. Retrieved March 6th, 2024.

15. Roll, David. *George Marshall: Defender of the Republic*. Caliber. New York, NY. 2019. Page 130.

16. "Desmond Tutu Quotes." *Good reads*. https://www.goodreads.com/quotes/132842-a-person-is-a-person-through-other-persons-none-of. Retrieved March 6th, 2024.

17. Cahn, Lauren. "The Untold Truth of Chick-Fil-A Founder S. Truett Cathy." *Mashed*. October 4th, 2020. https://www.mashed.com/256322/the-untold-truth-of-chick-fil-a-founder-s-truett-cathy/. Retrieved March 6th, 2024.

18. Economy, Peter. "Chick-fil-A Founder Reveals His Brilliant Secrets of Business and Life in Lost Interview *Inc*. December 7th, 2018. https://www.inc.com/peter-economy/chick-fil-a-founder-s-truett-

cathy-reveals-his-brilliant-secrets-of-success-in-business-life-in-lost-in-terview.html. Retrieved March 6th, 2024.

Chapter 5

1.   Singh, Abhijeet. "7 Warren Buffett quotes that may redefine your purpose of stock market investing." *Financial Express*. August 18th, 2018. https://www.financialexpress.com/market/7-warren-buffett-quotes-that-may-redefine-your-purpose-of-stock-market-investing-1284683/. Retrieved March 6th, 2024.

2.   Anderson, Somer. "How Does a Change in CEO Impact Stock Price? *Investopedia*. January 26th, 2023. https://www.in-vestopedia.com/ask/answers/010815/how-does-change-ceo-impact-stock-price.asp. Retrieved March 8th, 2024.

3.   Anderson, Somer. "What Short Interest Tells Us." *Investopedia*. March 23rd, 2022. https://www.investopedia.com/arti-cles/01/082201.asp. Retrieved March 8th, 2024.

4.   "7 Ways to Prepare Your Healthcare Business for Practice Expansion." *PNC Insights*. July 10th, 2023. https://www.pnc.com/in-sights/small-business/growing-your-business/7-ways-to-prepare-your-healthcare-business-for-practice-expansion.html. Retrieved March 8th, 2024.

Chapter 6

1.   "Importance of Revenue Generation." *Faster Capital.* https://fastercapital.com/startup-topic/Importance-of-Revenue-Generation.html. Retrieved March 8th, 2024.

2.   Altman, Ian. "The Good, The Bad, and The Ugly of Cost Cutting." *Forbes.* March 17th, 2015. https://www.forbes.com/sites/ianaltman/2015/03/17/the-good-the-bad-and-the-ugly-of-cost-cutting/?sh=846e795377b7. Retrieved March 8th, 2024.

Chapter 7

1.   Lane, Liz. "Healthcare Care Organization Financial Statements: Understanding Best Practices." *Richter HC.* April 14th, 2021. https://blog.richterhc.com/health-care-organization-financial-statements-understanding-best-practices. Retrieved March 11th, 2024.

2.   Shah, Riken. "7 Tips to Follow While Developing Financial Information System in Healthcare." *OSP.* https://www.osplabs.com/insights/7-tips-to-follow-while-developing-financial-information-system-in-healthcare/. Retrieved March 11th, 2024.

3.   Luther, David. "Healthcare Financial Management: An Expert Guide." *Oracle NetSuite.* https://www.netsuite.com/portal/resource/articles/financial-management/healthcare-financial-management.shtml. Retrieved March 11th, 2024.

Chapter 8

1.   "The Basics of Healthcare Budgeting and Capital Budgeting." Syntellis. https://www.syntellis.com/guide-to-healthcare-and-hospital-budgeting. Retrieved March 11th, 2024.

2.   Bichachi, Rebeca. "Healthcare & Hospital Budgeting Guide for 2024." January 3rd, 2024. https://www.netsuite.com/portal/re-source/articles/financial-management/healthcare-budgeting.shtml. Retrieved March 11th, 2024.

Chapter 9

1.   Ratcliffe, Susan. "Joel Arthur Barker American futurist." *Oxford Reference*. 2016.

2.   "In epic Super Bowl upset, Jets make good on Namath guarantee." *History*. https://www.history.com/this-day-in-history/super-bowl-upsets-joe-namath-1969. Retrieved March 11th, 2024.

3.   Woo, Ben. "Innovation Distinguishes Between A Leader And A Follower." *Forbes*. February 14th, 2013. https://www.forbes.com/sites/bwoo/2013/02/14/innovation-distin-guishes-between-a-leader-and-a-follower/?sh=46c168e28447. Retrieved March 11th, 2024.

4.   Dumonjic. Alen. "Football 101: Breaking Down the West Coast Offense." *Bleacher Report*. March 2nd, 2013. https://bleacherre-port.com/articles/1087386-football-101-breaking-down-the-west-coast-offense. Retrieved March 11th, 2024.

5.	"The Whole Is Greater Than The Sum Of Its Parts – Meaning, Origin & Usage (10+ Examples)" https://grammarhow.com/the-whole-is-greater-than-the-sum-of-its-parts-meaning/. Retrieved March 11th, 2024.

6.	U.S. hockey team beats the Soviets in the "Miracle on Ice." *History.* https://www.history.com/this-day-in-history/u-s-hockey-team-makes-miracle-on-ice. Retrieved March 11th, 2024.

7.	"Quote Origin: Success Is Never Final and Failure Never Fatal. It's Courage That Counts." September 3rd, 2013. https://quoteinvestigator.com/2013/09/03/success-final/. Retrieved March 11th, 2024.

8.	Rao, Carol. "Was Michael Jordan Really Cut from His High School Basketball Team?" *Sportscasting.* March 14th, 2020. https://www.sportscasting.com/was-michael-jordan-really-cut-from-his-high-school-basketball-team/. Retrieved March 11th, 2024.

9.	"The Socratic Method." https://www.socratic-method.com/quote-meanings-interpretations/ralph-waldo-emerson-to-know-even-one-life-has-breathed-easier-because-you-have-lived-this-is-to-have-succeeded-2. Retrieved March 11th, 2024.

10.	"Dan Millman Quotes." https://www.good-reads.com/quotes/2232590-the-secret-of-change-is-to-focus-all-your-energy. Retrieved March 11th, 2024.

Chapter 10

1.   "What Is Regulatory Compliance in Healthcare?" *Healthcare Compliance Pros.* https://www.healthcarecompliance-pros.com/blog/what-is-regulatory-compliance-in-healthcare. Retrieved March 21st, 2024.

2.   Harris, Tamrah Harris. "10 Best EHR Software (March 2024)." *Forbes Advisor.* https://www.forbes.com/advisor/business/software/best-ehr-software/. Retrieved March 21st, 2024.

3.   "Capital expenditure in the health sector." *OECDiLibrary.* https://www.oecd-ilibrary.org/sites/dba7d3b8-en/index.html?itemId=/content/component/dba7d3b8-en. Retrieved March 21st, 2024.

4.   Morgan, D. and R. Astolfi (2013), "Health Spending Growth at Zero: Which Countries, Which Sectors Are Most Affected?", OECD Health Working Papers, No. 60, OECD Publishing, Paris, https://dx.doi.org/10.1787/5k4dd1st95xv-en. Retrieved March 21st, 2024.

5.   Mueller, M. and D. Morgan (2018), Deriving preliminary estimates of primary care spending under the SHA 2011 framework, OECD, Paris, http://www.oecd.org/health/health-systems/Preliminary-Estimates-of-Primary-Care-Spending-under-SHA-2011-Framework.pdf. Retrieved March 21st, 2024.

6.   Mueller, M. and D. Morgan (2017), "New insights into health financing: First results of the international data collection under the

System of Health Accounts 2011 framework", Health Policy, Vol. 121/7, pp. 764-769, https://doi.org/10.1016/j.healthpol.2017.04.008.

7.   "Payor." *Definitive Healthcare*. https://www.definitivehc.com/resources/glossary/payor. Retrieved March 21ˢᵗ, 2024.

Chapter 11

1.   Beattie, Andrew. "Steve Jobs and the Apple Story: The legacy and lessons of Apple's co-founder." December 13ᵗʰ, 2022. *Investopedia*. https://www.investopedia.com/articles/fundamental-analysis/12/steve-jobs-apple-story.asp. Retrieved March 27ᵗʰ, 2024.

2.   Newman, Rick. "How Netflix (and Blockbuster) killed Blockbuster." *US News & World Report*. September 23ʳᵈ, 2010. https://money.us-news.com/money/blogs/flowchart/2010/09/23/how-netflix-and-blockbuster-killed-blockbuster. Retrieved March 27ᵗʰ, 2024.

3.   Feloni, Richard. "How Lego Came Back From the Brink of Bankruptcy." *Entrepreneur*. February 12ᵗʰ, 2014. https://www.entrepreneur.com/business-news/how-lego-came-back-from-the-brink-of-bankruptcy/231447. Retrieved March 27ᵗʰ, 2024.

4.   Growth, Aimee. "19 Amazing Ways CEO Howard Schultz Saved Starbucks." *Business Insider*. June 19ᵗʰ, 2011. https://www.businessinsider.com/howard-schultz-turned-starbucks-around-2011-6. Retrieved March 27ᵗʰ, 2024.

5. Agarwal, Meha. "Airbnb's Journey From a Failing Startup to a $25 Bn Company." *Inc42*. June 16th, 2016. https://inc42.com/resources/airbnbs-journey-failing-startup-25-bn-company/. Retrieved March 27th, 2024.

6. Ashmore, Dan. "Bitcoin Price History 2009 to 2022." *Forbes Advisor*. October 11th, 2022. https://www.forbes.com/advisor/investing/cryptocurrency/bitcoin-price-history/. Retrieved March 27th, 2024.

7. Pinkerton, Julie. "The History of Bitcoin, the First Cryptocurrency." *US News and World Report*. March 21st, 2024. https://money.usnews.com/investing/articles/the-history-of-bitcoin. Retrieved March 27th, 2024.

Chapter 12

1. Westover, Jonathan. "The Power of Listening." *Forbes*. August 17th, 2020. https://www.forbes.com/sites/forbescoachescouncil/2020/08/17/the-power-of-listening/?sh=32eb036f16a3. Retrieved March 27th, 2024.

2. "10 Quotes to Inspire Active Listening in The Workplace." *Robert Half*. May 26th, 2023. https://www.roberthalf.com/us/en/insights/career-development/10-quotes-to-inspire-active-listening. Retrieved March 27th, 2024.

3. Bradford, Carol. "The Power of Listening." *The Ohio State College of Medicine*. November 2020. https://medicine.osu.edu/ohio-state-

medicine-dr-bradford-message/november-2020. Retrieved March 27th, 2024.

Chapter 13

1.   Iwere, Ted. "4 Reasons Delegation Is Important for Business Success." *LinkedIn*. July 12th, 2023. https://www.linkedin.com/pulse/4-reasons-delegation-important-business-success-ted-iwere/. Retrieved April 13th, 2024.

2.   Atanacio, Alfredo. "The Importance of Delegating Effectively." *Forbes*. June 15th, 2020. https://www.forbes.com/sites/theyec/2020/06/15/the-importance-of-delegating-effectively/?sh=73eb6b4d791c. Retrieved April 13th, 2024.

3.   Loucks, Micah. "Importance of delegation in business." *MSU Extension*. December 8th, 2017. https://www.canr.msu.edu/news/importance_of_delegation_in_business. Retrieved April 13th, 2024.

4.   Grossman, David. "The 6 Benefits of Delegation and Why Most Leaders Under-Delegate." *The Grossman Group*. July 17th, 2023. https://www.yourthoughtpartner.com/blog/the-benefits-of-delegation-and-why-most-leaders-under-delegate. Retrieved April 13th, 2024.

5.   Landry, Lauren. "How to Delegate Effectively: 9 Tips for Managers." *HBS Online*. January 14th, 2020. https://online.hbs.edu/blog/post/how-to-delegate-effectively. Retrieved April 13th, 2024.

6.   Polzin, Roland. "5 Reasons Why Delegation is a Must for Entrepreneurs." *Entrepreneur*. February 2nd, 2023. https://www.entrepreneur.com/growing-a-business/5-reasons-why-effective-delegation-is-crucial-for/443326. Retrieved April 13th, 2024.

7.   Famakinwa, J.O. "Is the unexamined worth life worth living or not?" *Cambridge University Press*. Think , Volume 11 , Issue 31 , Summer 2012 , pp. 97 – 103.
DOI: https://doi.org/10.1017/S1477175612000073. Retrieved April 13th, 2024.

8.   "Friedrich Nietzsche Quotes." *Goodreads*. https://www.goodreads.com/quotes/22323-all-things-are-subject-to-interpretation-whichever-interpretation-prevails-at. Retrieved April 13th, 2024.

9.   Griffin, Jill. "Luck is What Happens When Preparation Meets Opportunity." *Forbes*. April 9th, 2019.
https://www.forbes.com/sites/jillgriffin/2019/04/09/luck-is-what-happens-when-preparation-meets-opportunity/?sh=2530bf6469c4. Retrieved April 13th, 2024.

10.   H. Jackson Brown Jr. Quotes.
https://www.brainyquote.com/quotes/h_jackson_brown_jr_133311. Retrieved April 13th, 2024.

11.   Esposito, Eva. "The Bus Metaphor." *Diplo Learning Corner*. January 22nd, 2020. https://diplolearn.org/2020/01/22/the-right-people-in-the-right-seats-on-the-bus/. Retrieved April 13th, 2024.

Chapter 14

1.   "Benjamin Disraeli." *Goodreads.* https://www.goodreads.com/quotes/6780997-man-is-only-truly-great-when-he-acts-from-the. Retrieved April 15th, 2024.

2.   Famakinwa, J.O. "Is the unexamined worth life worth living or not?" *Cambridge University Press.* Think , Volume 11 , Issue 31 , Summer 2012 , pp. 97 – 103. DOI: https://doi.org/10.1017/S1477175612000073. Retrieved April 15th, 2024.

3.   "Address at Rice University On The Nation's Space Effort, September 12th, 1962." *John F. Kennedy Presidential Library and Museum.* September 12th, 1962. https://www.jfklibrary.org/archives/other-resources/john-f-kennedy-speeches/rice-university-19620912. Retrieved April 15th, 2024.

4.   Russell, Nan. "Ethics and Trust at Work." *Psychology Today.* May 19th, 2017. https://www.psychologytoday.com/us/blog/trust-the-new-workplace-currency/201705/ethics-and-trust-at-work. Retrieved April 15th, 2024.